Published by the Anglican Consultative Council
16 Tavistock Crescent
London W11 1AP, UK

This second edition © Copyright 2022, The Anglican Consultative Council, ISBN 978-1-911007-36-4

First edition 2008

Typeset in Adobe Caslon Pro.

The Principles of Canon Law Common to the Churches of the Anglican Communion

Second Edition

2022

ELS Ecclesiastical Law Society

Acknowledgements

This revision of the *Principles* has been made possible by the visionary scholarship of Professor Norman Doe, the contributions of very many individuals from the world of Anglican canon law, the typesetting skills of the Revd Neil Vigers of the Anglican Communion Office, the assiduous copy-editing of Dr Fiona Little, the indexing talents of Dr Francis Young and the sponsorship of the Ecclesiastical Law Society. The revision process was overseen by the Centre for Law and Religion at Cardiff University. Particular thanks are due to the convenors of the 2021 reading groups around the world, who included Jon Baldwin, the Revd Dr Hannah Cleugh, the Revd Stephen Coleman, the Revd Matthew Esau, the Very Revd Stephen Farrell, the Very Revd Kelvin Holdsworth, the Revd Canon Michael Hughes and Kelvin Ng; and to the members of the revision committee: the Revd Dr Will Adam, Dr Renae Barker, Dr the Hon Moses Cheng, the Revd Russell Dewhurst, the Worshipful Professor Mark Hill QC, the Rt Revd Dr Vicentia Kgabe, Mary Kostel, Justice Rubie Nottage, Darren Oliver and the Ven Alan Perry.

Thanks are also due to the Anglican Consultative Council, as holders of the copyright of this document, and for publishing this revision. It should be noted that the authority of the *Principles* comes solely from the fact that they state what is held in common in the laws of the churches of the Anglican Communion, and the involvement of the Anglican Consultative Council (ACC) in publication does not indicate any additional centrally mandated authority over and above this.

Contents

Foreword

By the Most Reverend and Right Honourable Justin Welby, Archbishop of Canterbury.

The rapidly changing shape of the Anglican Communion fully justifies the publication of a second edition of this document, and we should be grateful to those who have done a great deal of work in preparing it. The Preface sets out the background in a helpful way as well as listing the members of the revision committee (it might just be noted that with over half of membership of the Anglican Communion coming from Africa, it is regrettable that there is only one person on the revision committee from that continent).

The Anglican Communion is found in over 165 countries and forty-two, shortly to be forty-three, provinces, which are themselves grouped into five regions of the world. Within the Anglican Communion there are more than 2,000 languages and cultures. Members of the Communion range from people who live in the hills of Papua New Guinea to those who work in the canyons of Wall Street.

To find any common principles of any form of law is already an achievement. The vast majority of the Communion, probably well over 99 per cent of its worshipping members, will have no interest whatsoever in canon law. However that does not mean it is unnecessary. I am especially struck by the first three principles set out. They include the statement that 'Law exists to assist a church in its mission and witness to Jesus Christ.' This affirms that law is not an end in itself, although that often seems to be the case. The document seeks to deal with the different understandings of some of the most fundamental institutions within the Anglican Communion, including, for example, the household and the principles of marriage.

So thank you to the committee for what must have been a remarkable amount of hard work, which will serve as an important focus for attention and reflection and, I hope, discussion and development within the Anglican Communion.

I will now attempt to make one or two reflections.

First, in the wider environment of the secular law of the State, the natural bias of something which includes a significant number of people from the United Kingdom, North America, and other former parts of the British Empire is towards the common law and the way in which the common law works in the understanding of the nature of law. The common law is one of the most significant exports resulting from the British Imperial era. It became an essential and, for those of us who have ever studied it, invaluable part of the societies in which the British were the rulers for any extended period. However, it is not universal.

The Commonwealth is fewer than seventy countries. As I have already said, the Anglican Communion covers more than 165. These will encompass widely differing philosophies about divine law and understandings of the role of law in society. Many will have hierarchical systems of authority, as we do in the United Kingdom, but with very varied presumptions as to the value of universal participation in decisions that affect every member of a body or every person in society. The civil law is as extensive as common law, with a very different derivation: in the case of civil law from Roman law, as adapted in Constantinople and the Byzantine Empire and especially dramatically codified in places like France under Napoleon.

Common law and civil law are deeply different philosophies of law. Those who, like myself, admire the system of common law see in it a far greater adaptability to a rapidly changing world and to exceptionally fluid interrelations between different cultures than can be found in a more codified system. That is why I welcome this document as setting out not rules but principles of law.

An additional and immensely important further complication comes from the structure of the Anglican Communion itself. As is remarked, it is a communion, not a church. Every member church of the Anglican Communion has its own constitution and canons. They vary extensively both in how they are understood and in how they are written. Principles that are common to all of them will be extremely hard to find, and there will be vanishingly small numbers of principles that are rigorously observed across the entire Anglican Communion.

Far from making this document less important, it renders it absolutely essential as a point from which there can be greater development and discussion of church order that is just, humane, and above all centred on the life of the Christian disciple, led by the Holy Spirit of God, in obedience to the Father.

One of the puzzles that has struck me very forcefully in recent times is how the institutional (and legal) life of a church can stray so far from the grace-filled liberty of the people of Christ. We are told by St Paul that we are not under the law but under grace, yet too often in the way we live with each other we abandon grace and hug the law to ourselves. Grace and law are not opposites, but complements. Law is necessary to provide order, but grace is indispensable in leading us to awed worship before the presence of Jesus Christ.

This document, dipped into, will illustrate the questions and the challenges that come from the systems and principles of canon law common to the churches of the Communion. It is not only for lawyers, but for all those who seek to understand the different influences on the complex ecosystem that is the Anglican Communion. The Anglican Communion is flexible and adaptive: no photograph or set of principles can capture it, for the moment they have been printed, it has already changed. Before too long, the third edition will be necessary in a healthy church that seeks both the order that canon law brings and the freedom to proclaim the Gospel afresh in each generation.

Preface

By the Revd Dr Will Adam, Deputy Secretary General of the Anglican Communion; the Revd Russell Dewhurst, Fellow of the Centre for Law and Religion, Cardiff University; and Darren Oliver, Legal Adviser to the Anglican Consultative Council

There is no single body of law binding on all those churches which are members of the Anglican Communion. Each church is autonomous and governed according to its own legal system. Nevertheless, the existence of this publication bears witness to the fact that there are principles of canon law which are common to the churches of the Anglican Communion, and which can be factually established by studying the law of the churches.

The genesis of the *Principles*

The development of the *Principles* can be traced to the Primates' Meeting (attended by the Primates of the Anglican Communion) at Kanuga, USA, in 2001. The legal academic Norman Doe presented a paper, based on his 1998 book *Canon Law in the Anglican Communion* and other research, on the unwritten common law shared by the member churches of the Communion. Wishing to explore these ideas further, the Primates' Meeting commissioned a Legal Advisers' Consultation from across the Communion, which responded positively to Professor Doe's hypothesis. At their meeting in Canterbury 2002, therefore, the Primates 'recognized that the unwritten law common to the churches of the Communion and expressed as shared principles of canon law may be understood to constitute a fifth "instrument of unity"' and endorsed the production of a draft statement of principles.

The Anglican Consultative Council accordingly established a Network of Legal Advisers in 2002 to produce a statement of shared principles. The Network formed a drafting group which met in 2005–8 to draft, discuss and revise principles taken initially from Norman Doe's work. The members of the drafting group were: Miss Philippa Amable, Chancellor of the Diocese of Ho, Province of Ghana; Mr David Booth Beers, Chancellor to the Presiding Bishop, Episcopal Church, United States; Mr Robert Falby, Chancellor of the Diocese of Toronto, Anglican Church of Canada; Mr Bernard Georges, Chancellor of the Province of the Indian Ocean; Mrs Rubie Nottage, Chancellor of the West Indies; Canon John Rees, Registrar of the Province of Canterbury, Church of England; Miss Fung-Yi Wong, Provincial Registrar of the Province of Hong Kong; and Canon Dr Gregory Cameron, Deputy Secretary General to the Anglican Consultative Council. As a result of the hard work of this group, in 2008 the Anglican Communion Office published *The Principles of Canon Law Common to the Churches of the Anglican Communion*. Further information on the initial process of development can be found in the preface of the 2008 Principles.

Reception and use of the *Principles*

In 2009 the Anglican Consultative Council commended *The Principles of Canon Law Common to the Churches of the Anglican Communion* for study in every province (Resolution 14.20).

The *Principles* have received considerable academic attention since their 2008 publication. A residential symposium, 'Canon Law in the Service of the Church', was held at the Anglican Centre in Rome in May 2010. A working party to study the *Principles* was set up by the Ecclesiastical Law Society (ELS), resulting in a lecture at Lincoln's Inn, London, in 2011. The *Principles* are now part of the syllabus of a Master of Laws degree course at Cardiff University—the LLM in Canon Law—whose alumni include lawyers, bishops, clergy, academics, church officers and others from across the Communion. The *Principles* were the subject of the 2019 Robin Sharwood Lecture by Professor Mark Hill QC at Trinity College, Melbourne, and St James Institute, Sydney. In the USA, they are regularly taught at Virginia Theological Seminary and were presented at a conference at Harvard Divinity School in 2015. They were the theme of a recent Church of Ireland clergy conference in the Diocese of Cork, Cloyne and Ross, and of numerous clergy seminars in several dioceses and provinces.

Articles published in academic journals have included Norman Doe's 'The Contribution of Common Principles of Canon Law to Ecclesial Communion in Anglicanism' (*Ecclesiastical Law Journal*, 2008) and Bishop Christopher Hill's 'Ecclesiological and Canonical Observations on *The Principles of Canon Law Common to the Churches of the Anglican Communion*' (*Ecclesiastical Law Journal*, 2012). Beyond the English language, an extensive treatment of the Anglican Principles by Professor Mark Hill QC can be found in *Dictionnaire du droit des religions* (CNRS Dictionnaires, 2011).

Churches of the Communion have made use of the *Principles* in the exposition and ongoing development of their canon law. For example, the *Diocesan Manual of Namibia* in the Anglican Church of Southern Africa quotes extensively from the *Principles*, which, it says, help the church 'to be clear and consistent about the function of Canon Law in the Anglican Communion'. The *Principles* have been available to give insights to new provinces in the formation of their law and to existing provinces in the development of their existing law.

Reference has also been made to the *Principles* in both ecclesiastical and secular courts worldwide. In re *Wangaratta Blessing Service* (2020), the majority of the Appellate Tribunal of the Anglican Church of Australia determined that they could not judge the legality of synodical legislation by reference to the *Principles*. This accords with the prediction made by John Rees in the 2008 preface to the *Principles*: 'if you try to rely on them in court as binding upon your own church, you are likely to come unstuck'. On the other hand, in *Bentley v. Anglican Synod of the Diocese of New Westminster* (2010) BCCA 506, the judgment of the Court of Appeal for British Columbia did grant some persuasive weight to the *Principles*, and specifically to the Part VII principles concerning church property.

Perhaps the most significant deployment of the *Principles* has taken place in the field of ecumenism. Because the Anglican Communion lacks a worldwide system of law, it was hitherto difficult in international gatherings to make general statements about Anglican law. As factual statements about canonical principles common to all the churches in the Communion, the *Principles* therefore fill a lacuna and facilitate ecumenical dialogue. For example, in the Colloquium of Anglican and Roman Catholic Canon Lawyers, a network of the Centre for Law and Religion at Cardiff University, Anglican members have begun to make ready use of the *Principles* in colloquia and published papers.

In 2017, *Walking Together on the Way*, an agreed statement of the Anglican–Roman Catholic International Commission, was published. Section VI.C proposes areas of receptive ecclesial learning at the worldwide levels of Anglican and Roman Catholic life, including a proposal that 'Anglicans could learn from the further development of canons, or commonly accepted canonical principles. Anglicans throughout the Communion could formally receive *The Principles of Canon Law Common to the Churches of the Anglican Communion*.' Furthermore, the Commission formed a judgment that commitment to the ethos of unity would also be strengthened by formal reception of the *Principles* (para. 158).

The methodology of the *Principles* inspired use as a model for the ecumenical Christian law principles project. A panel of experts was selected for their expertise in the church law, order or polity of particular Christian churches, Anglican, Baptist, Catholic, Lutheran, Methodist, Orthodox, Presbyterian and Reformed. Meeting annually from 2013, the panel formed the view that there are principles of Christian law, and a Statement of Principles of Christian Law was agreed in 2016. This work is currently being studied and utilised by the Faith and Order Commission of the World Council of Churches. The statement will be the subject of a workshop at the eleventh assembly of the World Council of Churches in 2022. The Statement of Principles, along with extensive discussion of the concept of legal principles across the churches, can be found in *Church Laws and Ecumenism: A New Path for Christian Unity* (2020), edited by Norman Doe.

Moreover, in the period since the first publication of the *Principles*, there has been a renewed understanding of the place of canon law in ecumenism. In 2019, Ecumenical Patriarch Bartholomeos I described the 2016 Statement of Principles of Christian Law as 'a means of unity and collaboration between Christians of different traditions, designed to fill the historic juridical deficit in the ecumenical enterprise'. In the same year, Pope Francis stated that 'canon law is essential for ecumenical dialogue' and that 'ecumenical dialogue also enriches canon law'. It is hoped that, in the years ahead, the *Principles* will continue to play their role in the growing canonical dimension of the ecumenical endeavour.

The 2022 revision of the *Principles*

By 2021, it was apparent that the law of the churches had continued to develop and that the *Principles* needed to be updated. There had, as yet, been only sporadic responses to the Anglican Consultative Council's resolution asking every member church to study the *Principles*, and so the ELS stepped into the breach. The ELS organised ten reading groups which gathered online over a period of several months to read and comment on the *Principles*. The groups' membership included over sixty ecclesiastical lawyers, bishops, clergy and academics from across the Anglican Communion, with a particular focus on Aotearoa, New Zealand and Polynesia; Australia; Canada; England; Hong Kong; Ireland; Scotland; and Southern Africa. The purpose of the groups was the edification of the participants, to strengthen Anglican bonds and also to provide data for the revision of the *Principles*. Each group submitted notes on principles which were found to be consistent or inconsistent with the law of their church, supported by detailed legal evidence and quotations from legal sources. The work of revision would have been impossible without the labours of this global community and the dedication of the groups' convenors.

The groups' findings, along with other evidence-based responses to the Principles which had been made over the years, were the primary source for the work of a new revision committee, formed in late 2021 under the aegis of the Centre for Law and Religion at Cardiff University.

For the record, membership of the revision committee was as follows:

The Revd Dr Will Adam
Deputy Secretary General of the Anglican Communion

Dr Renae Barker
Senior Lecturer, University of Western Australia, Diocesan Advocate of Bunbury

Dr the Hon Moses Cheng
Chancellor of the Hong Kong Sheng Kung Hui

The Revd Russell Dewhurst (chair)
Fellow and doctoral student, Cardiff Centre for Law and Religion

Professor Norman Doe
Director, Cardiff Centre for Law and Religion; Chancellor of Bangor

The Worshipful Professor Mark Hill QC
Cardiff Centre for Law and Religion; Chancellor of Chichester, Leeds and Gibraltar in Europe

The Rt Revd Dr Vicentia Kgabe
Bishop of Lesotho

Mary Kostel
Chancellor to the Presiding Bishop of The Episcopal Church

Justice Rubie Nottage
Former Provincial Chancellor, Church in The Province of the West Indies

Darren Oliver
Legal Adviser to the Anglican Consultative Council; Provincial Registrar of Canterbury

The Ven Alan Perry
General Secretary of the Anglican Church of Canada

The initial drafting of updated principles was undertaken by Norman Doe, using the findings of the reading groups and others. This drafting was followed by intensive debate and amendment on the part of the committee meeting several times over the course of January 2022.

Whenever churches legislate, what had previously been common to the churches may no longer be common. A church's act of legislation, therefore, may alter or subtract from the store of common principles. The revision committee found many examples of this in the course of the revision. If even just a small number of churches supplied information of laws contrary to a principle as previously formulated, that principle has accordingly been revised or removed to reflect this change.

Particular mention should be made of laws relating to matrimony. As of 2022, the law of most churches provides only for marriage between one man and one woman, whereas the law of some churches provides also for marriage between people of the same sex. After extensive discussion, and consultation with legal advisers across the Communion, the revision committee decided that a principle 'common to the Churches of the Anglican Communion' could not be found to encompass this diversity of legal provision. Principle 70, therefore, could not be presented in the same way as the other principles. In the case of every other revision, the revision committee was able to proceed by way of consensus. The text now included under Principle 70, by contrast, was agreed following majority voting and does not necessarily represent the views of all members of the committee.

Many other principles have been updated or amended. Principles which have been revised between 2008 and 2022 are listed in the Appendix of this publication.

Between 2016 and 2019, the Anglican Communion Safe Church Commission developed international guidelines to promote safeguarding best practice. The resultant *Guidelines to Enhance the Safety of All Persons—Especially Children, Young People and Vulnerable Adults—within the Provinces of the Anglican Communion* were approved by the Anglican Consultative Council in 2019. The *Principles* revision committee found this to be a significant development, but did not elucidate new principles for inclusion in this revision. The *Guidelines* are an example of the increasing prevalence of 'soft law' as a source of principles which are quasi-legal. Quasi-legal principles may accordingly be expected to play a growing role in the law of Anglican churches.

No new principles were added during the 2022 revision process. However, this is not ruled out for the future as laws continue to develop. For example, among the legal responses to the global COVID-19 pandemic, many churches have legislated, inter alia, to permit synodical bodies to meet virtually and to ensure that those unable to receive Holy Communion because of restrictions on gathering do not lose legal rights attached to communicant status. It may be that, in time, new common principles are able to be discerned where the laws of the churches have developed in parallel.

The draft revision of the *Principles* was circulated to as many churches' chief legal advisers as could be contacted for comment. Feedback was received from Aotearoa, New Zealand and Polynesia; Australia; Burundi; Canada; Central Africa; Ceylon; England; Hong Kong; Wales; West Africa; Sudan; and the USA. It was acknowledged that in most cases this feedback did not come from an official representative body of the church, but was the comment of one or more senior canon lawyers learned in the law of their province. The revision committee was very grateful to receive these comments, as a result of which further changes were made and the final version of *The Principles of Canon Law Common to the Churches of the Anglican Communion* 2022 was agreed.

The Anglican Communion Office arranged for the typesetting, publication and translation of the new *Principles*. Thanks to the ongoing support of the ELS for this project, the 2022 *Principles* contain a detailed index, intended to make the *Principles* even more accessible and useful for scholarly reference.

Definitions

Unless stated otherwise the term **'Anglican Communion'** refers to those churches listed in the schedule to the Constitution of the Anglican Consultative Council and those non-provincial churches or dioceses of which the Archbishop of Canterbury is Metropolitan.

'Assembly' means a representative assembly in a church, being a synod, council, convention or other assembly, which consists at national, regional or provincial level of bishops, clergy and laity, at diocesan level of the bishop, clergy and laity, and at parochial or other local level of clergy and laity.

Unless the context suggests otherwise, **'the bishop'** means the diocesan bishop.

'A church' means an autonomous member church, national, regional, provincial or extra-provincial, of the Anglican Communion.

Unless the context suggests otherwise, **'the church'** means the church universal.

The expression **'church universal'** means the One, Holy, Catholic and Apostolic Church.

The expression **'central church assembly'** means the highest representative and legislative authority within a church, which may have the title General Synod, General Convention, Provincial Council or other style.

'Civil law' means the secular laws of the territory where a church is situated.

'Clergy' means bishops, priests and deacons, unless the context suggests otherwise (such as when a principle distinguishes bishops and other clergy), in which case 'clergy' means priests and deacons.

An **'ecclesiastical authority'** is an ecclesiastical person who or institution which exercises jurisdiction or other binding decision-making function recognised by law within a church.

The expression **'general law of a church'** means the law of that body which has competent jurisdiction over that church, as distinct from laws of units within a church such as a diocese.

'Law' signifies 'church law', a binding public instrument created within a church by a duly constituted lawful authority of that church, that is, a species of human law as distinct from the will or law of God.

Unless the context suggests otherwise, the word **'may'** means that the person to whom, or body (including a church) to which, it applies has a permissive right, authority or other entitlement or power, subject to such conditions as may be prescribed by law, to choose whether act or not to act.

The word **'parish'** signifies a parish, pastorate, incumbency or other similar entity which represents the most localised ecclesiastical unit in a diocese.

The expression **'parish priest'** means an incumbent, rector, vicar or other ordained minister having charge of the care of souls in the parish.

A **'principle of canon law'** is a foundational proposition or maxim of general applicability which has a strong dimension of weight, is induced from the similarities of the legal systems of churches, derives from the canonical tradition or other practices of the church, expresses a basic theological truth or ethical value and is about, is implicit in or underlies canon law.

The expression **'to the extent provided by law'**, and any analogous expression, mean that the matter treated in the principle is subject to such limitations, conditions or qualifications as may be contained in the law of a church. For the avoidance of doubt: (1) the expression is part of and an element of the principle itself, not a freestanding exception to the principle; (2) the expression acknowledges that other elements of the principle may be present to a greater or lesser degree in the law of a church; (3) the expression, therefore, seeks to accommodate any differences that may exist between the laws of churches as they particularise the principle in the lives of churches; and (4) the expression respects the fact that the law of a church may be silent on a matter treated in the principle, and, where the law is silent, the principle is assumed to be consistent with the law of a church. The purpose of this definition is to convey the generality of a principle, to accommodate legal diversity in the Communion and to signal the fundamental requirement of the rule of law in church life. Depending on the context, the words may also mean 'to the extent provided by civil law'.

Part I: Church Order

In this section, the Principles *are introduced by reference to their wider context, considering the nature of, and necessity for, law in a world made by a God who has embedded concepts of justice in his creation, and who has made himself known in his Son Jesus Christ. God calls the Christian church to bear witness to this revelation of his creating and redeeming love, and empowers it by his loving Spirit.*

The scope, authority and limits of the laws which govern the churches are set out, and their sources are considered. These laws seek to be a reflection of the will of God, providing a framework for the ongoing life of the Church as a human institution. They are never the last word in determining the will of God, though they will often encapsulate the accumulated wisdom and discernment of people living within a certain Christian tradition during the church's long history.

The laws of particular Anglican Churches can be factually established; from these can be deduced a body of underlying principles, to which each church contributes through its own legal system. These principles have a living force, and contain in themselves the possibility for further development; and the existence of these principles both demonstrates unity and may serve to promote unity within the Anglican Communion.

Principle 1: Law in ecclesial society

1. Law exists to assist a church in its mission and witness to Jesus Christ.

2. A church needs within it laws to order, and so facilitate, its public life and to regulate its own affairs for the common good.

3. Law is not an end in itself.

Principle 2: Law as servant

1. Law is the servant of the church.

2. Law should reflect and not be inconsistent with the revealed will of God.

3. Law has a historical basis and a theological foundation, rationale and end.

4. Law is intended to express publicly the theological self-understanding and practical policies of a church.

5. Law in a church exists to uphold the integrity of the faith, sacraments and mission, to provide good order, to support communion among the faithful, to put into action Christian values and to prevent and resolve conflict.

Principle 3: The limits of law

1. Laws should reflect but cannot change Christian truths.

2. Laws do not encompass all facets of ecclesial life.

3. Laws cannot prescribe the fullness of ecclesial life, ministry and mission.

4. Laws function predominantly in the public sphere of church life.

5. The principal subjects with which laws deal are ecclesiastical government, ministry, discipline, doctrine, liturgy, rites, property and ecumenical relations.

6. Some laws articulate immutable truths and values.

Principle 4: The sources and forms of law

1. Scripture, tradition and reason are fundamental authoritative sources of law.

2. The laws of churches exist in a variety of formal sources which should be identifiable, including constitutions, canons, rules, regulations and other instruments.

3. Historical sources recognised as such in the canonical tradition, including custom, have such status within a church as may be prescribed by its law.

4. Laws contain principles, norms, standards, policies, directions, rules, precepts, prohibitions, powers, freedoms, discretions, rights, entitlements, duties, obligations, privileges and other juridical concepts.

5. Laws should be short, clear and simple to the extent that is consistent with their purpose, meaning and comprehensiveness.

Principle 5: The rule of law

1. The law binds the bishops, clergy and lay officers.

2. The law may bind laypersons who do not hold office.

3. No one shall be above the law. All institutions and persons in positions of authority or office, ordained and lay, shall act in accordance with law.

4. Laws, rights and duties are enforceable within a church by its own ecclesiastical authorities through executive action or by judicial process.

5. Any person or body injured by a violation of law should be able to obtain a remedy before a competent ecclesiastical authority in accordance with the law.

6. A voluntary declaration, or other form of assent prescribed by law, to comply with ecclesiastical jurisdiction, binds the person who makes that declaration.

Principle 6: The requirement of authority

1. Ecclesiastical persons and bodies require authority to act.

2. Acts performed by those in ecclesiastical office and by ecclesiastical institutions carry the authority explicitly or implicitly conferred by the law.

3. Laypersons who do not hold ecclesiastical office are free, subject to their own consciences, to perform any act not prohibited by the law.

Principle 7: The applicability of law

1. Later laws abrogate earlier laws.

2. Laws are prospective and should not be retrospective in effect unless this is clearly provided for in the laws themselves.

3. Laws cannot oblige a person to do the impossible.

4. Persons cannot give what they do not have.

5. Laws should be applied in the service of truth, justice and equity.

6. Laws may be dispensed with in their application to particular cases on the basis of legitimate necessity provided authority to dispense is clearly given by the law.

Principle 8: The interpretation of law

1. Laws should be interpreted by reference to their text and context.

2. Laws are to be understood according to the proper meaning of their words.

3. Authoritative interpretations of law may be issued by church courts or tribunals, or by commissions or other bodies designated to interpret the law, in such cases, in such manner and with such effect as may be prescribed by the law.

4. If in a church the meaning of laws remains in doubt recourse may be had to analogous texts, the purposes and circumstances of the law, the mind of the legislator, the jurisprudence of church courts and tribunals, the opinion of jurists, the principles of canon law and theology, the common good and the practice and tradition of that church and of the church universal.

Principle 9: Juridical presumptions

1. Validity is acquired by full conformity to the will of God and is presumed by conformity to law.

2. Ordained ministries, validly conferred according to the gospel, the catholic tradition and the law of a church, are given by God as instruments of grace and possess not only the inward call of the Spirit, but also the commission of Christ through his body, the church universal.

3. Episcopal ministry, personal and collegial, is maintained, embodied and exercised in a variety of forms, under the law, in continuity of apostolic life and mission.

Part II: The Anglican Communion

The Anglican Communion is famously held together by 'bonds of affection' in the absence of any central juridical authority. But there is a legal underpinning, highly dispersed and diverse, which constitutes a remarkably resilient web of relationships reinforcing the relationships between the churches that are linked historically with the ministry of the See of Canterbury.

This legal underpinning finds expression notably in mutual recognition of ministry and orders within the churches of the Communion, and in mutual eucharistic hospitality between the members of the constituent churches. In each case, such matters are governed by the legal and constitutional provisions in each church.

The strict legal autonomy of each church is seen not as an end in itself, but as a means to provide 'the greatest possible liberty to order its life and affairs, appropriate to its people in their geographical, cultural and historical context' in living in interdependence with other Anglican churches who share the same historic identity and calling.

The churches of the Anglican Communion remain in communion with the See of Canterbury. The relationship of communion is served by four instruments of communion, namely the Archbishop of Canterbury, the Lambeth Conference, the Primates' Meeting and the Anglican Consultative Council. Each of these enjoys the degree of binding authority (if any) given to them by each of the churches.

Principle 10: The fellowship of the Anglican Communion

1. The Anglican Communion is a fellowship of churches within the One, Holy, Catholic and Apostolic Church, characterised by their historic relationship of communion with the See of Canterbury.

2. The churches of the Anglican Communion are duly constituted national, regional, provincial churches and dioceses, and uphold and propagate the historic faith and order as typified in the Book of Common Prayer 1662 and its derivatives authorised in the several churches of the Communion.

3. The relationship of ecclesial communion within the Anglican Communion is based on the communion of a church with one or more of the following: (a) the See of Canterbury; (b) the Church of England; (c) all the churches of the Anglican Communion; (d) all churches in communion with the See of Canterbury; (e) all churches which profess the apostolic faith as received within the Anglican tradition.

Principle 11: The instruments of communion

1. Each church acknowledges its adherence to Holy Scripture as containing all things necessary to salvation, the Apostles' and Nicene Creeds, the sacraments of baptism and eucharist, the historic episcopate, the threefold ministry of bishops, priests and deacons, and common patterns of worship.

2. Each church recognises that the churches of the Anglican Communion are bound together, not juridically by a central legislative, executive or judicial authority, but by mutual loyalty maintained through the instruments of Anglican unity as an expression of that communion.

3. The relationship between member churches is governed morally by the conventions of the Anglican Communion and juridically by the law of each church.

4. The unity of the Anglican Communion is served by four instruments of communion, namely the Archbishop of Canterbury, the Lambeth Conference, the Primates' Meeting and the Anglican Consultative Council.

5. The instruments of communion enjoy such binding authority within a church as may be prescribed by the law of that church.

Principle 12: Autonomy and interdependence

1. Each church is autonomous in respect of its freedom of self-government.

2. Each autonomous church is free to order and regulate its affairs through its own system of government and law.

3. The validity within a church of any ecclesiastical act is governed by the law of that church in which the act is performed.

4. The exercise within a church of any ecclesiastical function is governed by the law of that church in which the function is exercised.

5. No church is legally bound by a decision of any ecclesiastical body external to itself, unless that decision is authorised under or incorporated into its own law.

6. A church may impose by its own law restraints on the exercise of its freedom of self-governance.

7. Each autonomous church has the greatest possible liberty to order its life and affairs, taking into consideration appropriateness to its people in their geographical, cultural and historical context, and compatibility with its belonging to and interdependence with the church universal.

Principle 13: Mutual respect

1. A church shall respect the autonomy of each church in the Anglican Communion.

2. Each church and its individual members should respect a legislative, executive, judicial or other decision or action duly authorised under the law of another church.

3. No church, or any authority or person within it, shall intervene in the internal affairs of another church without the consent of that other church given in such manner as may be prescribed by its own law.

4. It is within the jurisdiction of the central assembly of a church to regulate relationships between that church and other churches of the Anglican Communion.

5. The law of each church provides that the Word of God be authentically preached, and the sacraments of baptism and eucharist be duly administered.

Principle 14: Mutual hospitality

1. Each church in the Anglican Communion welcomes members of all other churches in the Communion to share in the spiritual benefits available in the host church.

2. Each church should provide pastoral care and ministrations to a visiting member of a fellow church in the Communion.

3. Each church should admit to Holy Communion a visiting member of a fellow church in the Communion to the extent authorised by the law of the host church.

4. Each church should welcome the participation in its public worship of a visiting member of a fellow church in accordance with the law of the host church.

5. Each church recognises as between the churches of the Anglican Communion the interchangeability of ministers ordained in a fellow church in the Communion to the extent authorised by the law of the host church.

6. Interchangeability of ordained ministers excludes re-ordination.

7. Ministerial interchangeability enables a minister of one church to exercise ministry in another, and its enjoyment requires the minister to obtain prior permission of the competent authorities of both churches and to comply with the law of the host church.

Part III: Ecclesiastical Government

This section of the Principles *not only addresses the institutional organisation to be found in churches of the Anglican Communion, but also sets out some of the just legal principles which the Communion recognises as applicable in governance by them.*

The Old Testament reminds us that counsel and sound judgment come from God and that laws that are just flow from that source (Proverbs 8.14–15). The traditional organisation of the churches of the Communion is included in this section. Parishes, dioceses and provinces are recognised by this section as the common institutions of each church.

The Principles *confirm that the exercise of ecclesiastical governance is to be characterised by Christian virtues, transparency and the rule of law, which is to be applied with justice and equity within the institutions of a church and by those persons exercising authority. These include accountability, appropriate representation, legislative authority, natural justice, due process and the appropriate participation of each of the orders of bishops, clergy and laity.*

In the 2022 revision, Principle 15.11, which had previously referred to collegiality alone, was changed to 'Episcopacy is exercised personally, collegially and communally.' This uses the language of the Lambeth Conference 1988, the Porvoo agreement and the World Council of Churches' 'Baptism, Eucharist and Ministry' as a fuller description of the exercise of episcopacy.

Principle 15: Ecclesiastical polity

1. A church is an autonomous territorial unit of ecclesiastical jurisdiction.

2. A church may be a national, regional, provincial or extra-provincial unit.

3. A national or a regional church may consist of more than one province. A province consists of dioceses. A diocese may consist of parishes or other localised ecclesiastical units.

4. A province within a national or regional church enjoys such status within it as may be provided by the general law of that church.

5. An extra-provincial church is organised on a diocesan basis and is not part of a province but may come under metropolitical jurisdiction in another church.

6. Each church, province and diocese has an assembly, namely a synod, council or other body, the function of which is to govern. A parish also has an assembly.

7. The relationship between a church and the ecclesiastical units within it is regulated by the general law of that church.

8. The relationship between the central assembly of a church and the assemblies of the ecclesiastical units within it is regulated by the general law of that church.

9. Bishops, clergy and laity of a church share authority in synodical government.

10. Episcopacy is fundamental to church polity.

11. Episcopacy is exercised personally, collegially and communally.

12. The exercise of ecclesiastical governance should be characterised by the Christian virtues, transparency and the rule of law applied with justice and equity.

13. Laws should set out clearly the composition of, powers of and limitations on the exercise of powers by ecclesiastical institutions, their relationship one to another and the rights and duties of those who hold office and of the faithful generally.

14. The transaction of business in any church assembly must be in accordance with such standing orders or other procedures as are lawfully established for that assembly.

Principle 16: Leadership and authority

1. Leadership and authority are gifts of God, their exercise mediated through a church.

2. Jurisdiction may be exercised by ecclesiastical persons or institutions.

3. Persons who have jurisdiction, or an office or other position in church government, ordained and lay, exercise leadership and authority on behalf of a church.

4. Leadership and authority should be exercised in an accountable manner, within the episcopal and synodical structures of a church, with respect for

others in authority and with regard for the common good and the dignity, rights, needs and gifts of all.

5. Persons who exercise ecclesiastical governance should work in a collaborative and cooperative manner with those whom they encounter in their ministry and must not act arbitrarily but give, as appropriate, reasons for their decisions.

6. Persons who exercise ecclesiastical governance, as agents of healing and reconciliation, are to be a visible sign of unity and should not jeopardise that unity or be the cause or focus of division and strife by the exercise of their leadership.

Principle 17: Administration

1. Effective ministry requires efficient administration.

2. Ecclesiastical institutions and persons must ensure that their administrative practices are lawful, competent and courteous.

3. Vision and preparation, decision and action, and communication, consultation and cooperation are key elements of good ecclesiastical administration.

4. Bodies which or persons who exercise ecclesiastical functions may delegate to others only such functions as they are not required to perform themselves provided the delegation is carried out with care, with the consent of those to whom the function is delegated and in the manner and to the extent prescribed by law.

Principle 18: Representative government

1. Representative government is fundamental to church polity, and in matters which touch all, all should have a voice.

2. The central assembly of a church, and the assembly of a province or diocese, consist of bishops, clergy and laity.

3. Central, provincial and diocesan assemblies consist of houses, orders or other cameral systems which represent their episcopal, clerical and lay character.

4. A person must be qualified for, and elected or admitted to, membership of a church assembly in accordance with the law applicable to the ecclesiastical unit in which the assembly is located.

5. Diocesan bishops are members of church assemblies by virtue of their office, and other bishops should be represented in such assemblies as prescribed by law.

6. An episcopal synod or college, or other assembly of bishops, enjoys such authority as is recognised by law.

Principle 19: Legislative competence and subsidiarity

1. The power to legislate is vested in the representative assemblies of a church.

2. The central assembly of a church may have a general authority to legislate for the whole of that church within its territorial boundaries. In national or regional churches, legislative authority may be found in the

central assembly, assemblies of internal provinces or diocesan assemblies as the law provides.

3. An assembly of a church may introduce, amend or repeal law subject to the substantive and procedural limitations set by law.

Principle 20: The diocese and diocesan legislation

1. A diocese consists of the faithful in a particular territory overseen by a bishop.

2. Dioceses are to associate in provinces in accord with ancient usages of the church.

3. Formation, alteration or suppression of a diocese is in the keeping of the central church assembly and may be effected in such cases and manner as are allowed by law.

4. A see becomes vacant on the death, resignation, retirement or removal of its bishop.

5. The diocesan assembly, namely synod, council or other such body, may have authority to legislate for the diocese.

6. A diocesan bishop may give or withhold consent to proposed diocesan legislation to such extent as is provided by law, but may not legislate unilaterally.

Principle 21: The parish and parochial administration

1. The most local unit of a diocese is the parish or other similar ecclesiastical entity.

2. The formation, alteration or dissolution of a parish is in the keeping of the diocesan assembly, subject to provisions applicable under the general law of a church.

3. A parish is committed by the bishop to the spiritual care of an ordained minister.

4. A parish has a representative assembly which consists of clergy and laypersons.

5. Lay members of a parish assembly are selected or appointed by way of election or other lawful process from such classes of qualified persons as are prescribed by law.

6. The parish assembly has such functions as are prescribed by law to promote the whole mission of the church, pastoral, evangelistic, social and ecumenical.

7. A parish assembly or its officers may be required to report annually to the diocesan authorities on matters affecting that parish.

Principle 22: Lay participation in government

1. Laypersons are entitled to participate in the governance of a church.

2. A church must enable lay participation in governance by provision for lawful admission to membership of its assemblies and other institutions of government.

3. Lay participation in church government is subject to the conditions prescribed in the law of a church as to eligibility, membership, selection and admission.

4. Communicant status is a normal requirement of eligibility for admission to the institutions and assemblies of government in a church.

5. Duly qualified laypersons may be chosen as representatives of laity for assemblies of government at all levels of a church in the manner prescribed by law.

Principle 23: Visitation

1. Visitation enables the exercise of a supervisory jurisdiction or a pastoral ministry, including enquiry into and assessment of the condition of an ecclesiastical entity.

2. Visitation may be exercised by the primate, archbishop, bishop or other ecclesiastical person to the extent authorised by the law.

3. Only those ecclesiastical entities may be visited which are prescribed by law.

4. Visitations may be held at such intervals, in such form and with such consequences as may be prescribed under the law.

Principle 24: Due judicial process

1. Ordinary jurisdiction in matters of discipline rests either with the bishop or with such other ecclesiastical person, court or tribunal as may be prescribed by law.

2. Church disputes must be resolved equitably, and in the first instance, the parties should seek to resolve their differences amicably.

3. Church courts and tribunals are to be available as necessary to resolve disputes.

4. The relationship between courts or tribunals of original and appellate jurisdiction in the judicial hierarchy is to be clearly prescribed by law.

5. The subject-matter jurisdiction of church courts and tribunals in disciplinary and other matters is to be clearly set out in the law.

6. Church courts or tribunals exercise jurisdiction in relation to and are to be accessible to such of the faithful, ordained or lay, as may be prescribed by law.

7. Judicial and other members of church courts and tribunals are to be duly qualified, selected and appointed by a designated ecclesiastical authority in accordance with a prescribed procedure, and are to exercise their office impartially, without fear or favour.

8. Church courts and tribunals are to enjoy independence from external interference and uphold the rule of law in the church.

9. In disciplinary cases, ecclesiastical offences are to be clearly defined and set out in writing.

10. In disciplinary and other cases in church courts or tribunals, the procedure is at all times to be fair and just, and is to protect rights of the parties to notice of proceedings, to adequate time for preparation of defence, to a presumption of innocence, to be heard within a reasonable time, to question evidence, to representation and to appeal in appropriate cases on a matter of fact or law.

11. Penalties or other forms of censure which may be imposed following proceedings in church courts or tribunals are to be clearly set out in the written law of a church.

12. Church courts and tribunals must give their decisions, and the reasons for them, in writing, and both decisions and reasons must be based on fact and law.

13. The decision of a church court or tribunal in a case binds the parties in that case.

14. The decision of a church court or tribunal has such binding or persuasive authority for other church courts or tribunals as may be provided for in the law.

15. Customary censures include deposition, deprivation, suspension, inhibition, admonition and rebuke.

Part IV: Ministry

This section sets out the scope and substance of the ministry of Anglican Christians in engaging, enabling and enlisting human resources in service of their mission to the world, promotion of fellowship of the faithful and witness to the gospel. All members are reminded of the call and cost of discipleship of Jesus Christ.

As indicated in previous sections, there are well-defined structures of governance, authority and responsibilities for the different roles and functions of its members, lay and ordained. These are contained in constitutions, canons and other legal instruments in different provinces and dioceses of the Communion, but all exist for the purpose of furthering God's mission in the world.

In spite of the diversity in culture and language in different parts in the Communion, there is a shared commitment of clergy and laity alike to support public and individual ministry, through ordained officials and lay members, the threefold ordained ministry of bishops, priests and deacons, and archiepiscopal and metropolitical authority. There are underlying principles of pastoral care, issues of professional and personal relationships, issues of confidentiality and, above all, recognition that all who minister should do so 'with respect and compassion'.

The 2008 iteration of this document included the following as a principle: 'Special provision may be made for parishes which in all conscience cannot accept the ministry of their own bishop for elements of episcopal ministry to be provided by another bishop as agreed from time to time with the diocesan bishop concerned' (Principle 38.5). There was insufficient legal commonality to include this in the current iteration.

Principle 25: The laity

1. All the faithful, in a manner appropriate to their state, participate in the tasks of teaching, governing and sanctifying.

2. The *laos* is the whole people of God, but for the purposes of law, a layperson is a person who is not in holy orders.

3. Laypersons exercise authority in church life and governance according to law.

4. The laity are subject to discipline to the extent and in the manner prescribed by law.

Principle 26: Fundamental rights and duties of the faithful

1. All persons are equal in dignity before God.

2. All persons have inherent rights and duties inseparable from their dignity as human beings created in the image and likeness of God and called to salvation through Jesus Christ.

3. Baptism is the foundation of Christian rights and duties.

4. A church should respect rights and duties founded on the dignity of the human person and on baptism as well as those afforded by ecclesiastical authority.

5. The church is concerned with the welfare of people in all its aspects, physical, mental and spiritual, and should as far as possible respond to the needs of all.

6. All the faithful, lay and ordained, by virtue of baptism, are responsible for church life and witness in the places where they live, and should: (a) regularly attend public worship, especially at Holy Communion; (b) practise daily devotion, private prayer, Bible reading and self-discipline; (c) bring the teaching and example of Christ into everyday life; (d) uphold Christian values; (e) be of personal service to church and community; and (f) assist the church financially in its work and mission.

7. All the faithful, ordained and lay, enjoy in a church such rights to government, ministry, teaching, worship, sacraments, rites and property as may flow from their human dignity, baptism, the duties of others and the law of that church.

8. In a church there is to be no unlawful denial of equal rights, status or access to the life, membership, government, ministry, worship, rites and property of that church on grounds of race, colour, ethnic, tribal or national origin, marital status, sex, sexual orientation, disability or age.

9. The faithful may freely associate in a religious order or other society which enjoys autonomy to establish and administer for its life in community its own rule, statutes or other constitution. The relationship between an order or society and a church is governed by the mutual acceptance of their respective regulatory systems.

10. All the faithful should recognise the unique status and needs of children and young people as a particularly vulnerable group, and a church should make such provision as is necessary to ensure their special protection. Mistreatment of children, especially their sexual abuse, offends their humanity and the teaching of Christ.

11. A church should provide for the affirmation and development of the ministry of all the baptised and should have, at the appropriate level, a commission or other body to promote these, the composition and functions of which may be prescribed by law.

Principle 27: Church membership

1. A church should serve, in appropriate ways, all who seek its ministry, regardless of membership.

2. Membership in a church, for the purposes of participation in its governance, may be based, as the case may be under its law, on any or all of these: baptism; baptism and confirmation; baptism, confirmation and communicant status; and regular attendance at public worship.

3. A church may receive into its membership any person who qualifies under its law.

4. A communicant member is a person who has received Holy Communion at such frequency and on such occasions as may be prescribed by law.

5. A communicant in good standing is a communicant who for a prescribed period has been faithful in worship and has supported the work and mission of the church.

6. Names of persons may be entered on a parish roll or other register of membership, subject to such conditions as may be prescribed by law, enabling eligibility for selection to participate in governance and other ecclesiastical functions and offices.

7. Names may be removed from a parish roll or other register of eligible voters in accordance with the law and observing the principles of justice and equity.

8. Membership of a church implicitly involves profession of the faith, acceptance of the doctrines of a church, submission to its government and law and the enjoyment of the fundamental and other rights and duties of the faithful.

Principle 28: Service in public ministry

1. Ministry is a gift of God exercised by persons, called by God and recognised as such by lawful authority, to serve the church in its mission and witness to the gospel.

2. Public ministry, ordained and lay, is the fulfilment of a function assigned formally in a church to an office or other position exercised under episcopal authority on behalf of that church in the service of its mission and in witness to the gospel.

3. Public ministry, lived out in its various forms, is exercised in a church as a structured community and institution, with organisation and standards, to promote the communion of the faithful and the mission of the church to the world.

4. Public ministry must be duly authorised in a church to sanctify, teach and oversee the community of faith, through its bodies and officers, and is exercised on behalf of that church in a representative capacity. People are entrusted with ministry.

5. Ministers have an accountable and professional role, calling for special competence and care, as defined in responsibilities and relationships by ordination, or other admission to office, and by a polity which exists to serve the integrity of the church.

Principle 29: Ecclesiastical office

1. Ecclesiastical offices include the offices of primate, archbishop, bishop, dean, archdeacon, parish priest, chancellor, registrar and warden.

2. An ecclesiastical office is a stable substantive position constituted by law, exists independently of the person who occupies it, enables the discharge of functions of the particular public ministry attaching to it and may be held in succession by its holders.

3. Ecclesiastical offices may be held by persons with such qualifications as are prescribed by the law, which may reserve some offices to ordained persons and provide that others may be held either by laypersons only or by ordained or lay persons, depending on the public ministry attaching to the office.

4. Admission to ecclesiastical office must be with the free consent of the candidate, by competent ecclesiastical authority and in accord with such process of conferral, installation, election or other form of appointment as is prescribed by law.

5. The jurisdiction or other authority which attaches to an office is determined by the ecclesiastical authority which established it, by the character of the office and by the law; authority attaching to an office may be delegated to the extent provided by law.

6. The exercise of ecclesiastical office is regulated by law, the requirements of leadership and authority, and the professional ethic of public ministry.

7. The authority to exercise ecclesiastical office is lost by lawful dissolution of the office, expiration of the stated term of office, attainment of the prescribed age limit or the death, resignation, transfer, retirement or removal of the office holder.

Principle 30: Lay ministry and offices

1. The law should prescribe: the qualifications necessary for a person to be authorised to exercise lay ministry or office; the procedure for, body giving and form of such authorisation; the functions and the manner in which they may be performed; and a fair process and authority competent to review, renew or terminate the exercise of such ministry or office.

2. To be eligible for admission to lay ministry or office, a person must satisfy such qualifications and other requirements as may be prescribed by the law.

3. Appointment to lay ministry or office is by lawful selective process, not as of right.

4. Lay ministers and officers are called to a public and representative ministry within and on behalf of a church with such functions as may be prescribed under its law.

5. Authority to minister may be limited by any or all of the following: the nature of the functions authorised to be performed; the person or body at whose request or by whose authority the functions may be performed; and the place at which and the period during which the functions may be performed.

6. The tenure of a lay ministry or office terminates on expiry of its term, on the death, resignation, retirement, removal of or withdrawal of authority from the person or as otherwise prescribed by law.

7. The authority to discipline, dismiss or reappoint a lay minister or officer is dependent on, and its exercise must comply with, the law.

8. Eligible laypersons may be admitted to such national, regional, provincial and diocesan offices as chairperson, chancellor, secretary, registrar or treasurer.

9. Eligible laypersons in a parish may be admitted to such ministries or offices as warden, steward, secretary, treasurer, reader, evangelist, eucharistic assistant, catechist, lector, pastoral assistant or other worker.

10. A warden or steward is selected in the parish, is admitted by due process, represents the laity, provides the necessities for and keeps order at public worship, and assists in the mission and ministry of the parish and in the administration and management of church property.

11. A lay communicant may be authorised by the bishop to exercise ministry as a reader, evangelist, eucharistic assistant, catechist, pastoral assistant or worker, under the direction of the relevant designated local clergy.

12. A reader is a layperson who may be authorised to: assist at public worship by reading, preaching, receiving and presenting the offerings of the people; regularly lead public worship, distribute the Holy Communion, conduct funerals, visit the sick, undertake pastoral and educational work; and otherwise support clergy as the bishop may direct.

13. A lay eucharistic assistant is a layperson authorised to distribute the Holy Communion in church and, in the absence of sufficient clergy, to the sick.

14. A catechist is a layperson authorised to prepare persons for baptism, confirmation, reception and the reaffirmation of baptismal vows.

15. A lector is a layperson authorised by a member of the clergy in charge of a congregation to read the Word of God and to lead prayers.

16. A register of lay ministers and officers should be kept and maintained by the appropriate ecclesiastical authority.

Principle 31: Threefold ordained ministry

1. Ordained ministry is exercised by a person in holy orders.

2. The orders are bishops, priests and deacons.

3. Threefold ordained ministry accords with the practice and tradition of the church.

4. No person may be accepted in a church as a lawful bishop, priest or deacon, or allowed to perform any function belonging to these orders, unless ordained according to the appropriate rite authorised by or recognised under the law of that church.

5. A bishop has oversight to govern, teach and minister, a priest shares with and assists the bishop in the care of souls, and a deacon assists these; all are called to fulfil a ministry appropriate to their particular order.

6. Those in holy orders shall conduct their ministries in accord with the values enshrined in the law of their church and the practice of the church universal.

7. Bishops, priests and deacons are subject to the disciplinary jurisdiction of the courts or tribunals of a church.

8. The efficacy of a sacrament is not affected by the worthiness of its minister.

Principle 32: Ordination: the holy orders of priests and deacons

1. No person shall be admitted to holy orders unless called, tried, examined and admitted according to the rite of ordination.

2. The diocesan bishop has a special responsibility, with assistance from the faithful, to provide sufficient priests and deacons and to foster vocations to ordained ministry.

3. There is no right to ordination.

4. Baptism and confirmation are necessary qualifications for admission to holy orders.

5. The authority to determine suitability of a candidate for ordination as priest or deacon rests with the bishop subject to such limitations as may be prescribed by law.

6. The bishop must be satisfied that a candidate has the spiritual, moral, physical and mental qualities necessary for ordination and the exercise of ordained ministry.

7. The law determines the requirements for eligibility and qualifications of candidates for ordination, but some such requirements may be dispensed with by the archbishop or other designated authority to the extent permitted by law.

8. Men and women may be ordained to the extent permitted by law.

9. Progression from the diaconate to the priesthood is not automatic.

10. A church may provide for a permanent diaconate.

11. Prior to ordination, a candidate must submit to the diocesan bishop such evidence of eligibility and qualification as is required by law.

12. An ordination candidate must assent to church doctrine, and undertake to use only lawful forms of service, to obey the lawful and honest directions of the bishop and to comply with the law.

13. Ordination must take place in accordance with the ordinal or other authorised form of service for ordination as prescribed by law.

14. Ordination is administered episcopally under the authority of the diocesan bishop.

15. Valid ordination consists in fulfilment of what the church universal intends with the free consent of the candidate through the imposition of hands by a validly consecrated bishop with the invocation of the Holy

Spirit to give grace for the work of a priest or deacon, whichever particular order is bestowed.

16. An ordination cannot be repeated; orders are indelible.

Principle 33: The ministry of deacons and priests

1. A deacon has special responsibilities to care for people in need, and to assist the priest in proclamation of the gospel, in administration of public worship and in such other functions as are prescribed under the law.

2. When serving as an assistant in a parish, a deacon must act in accordance with the lawful directions of the person responsible for the care of souls therein.

3. A deacon must not exercise functions reserved to the order of priests.

4. A priest has a special responsibility, working with the bishop as servant and shepherd, to proclaim the gospel through preaching, teaching, administration of the sacraments and pastoral care.

5. The functions of priests include delivering sermons, presiding at the eucharist, pronouncing the absolution, visiting those within their charge, providing opportunities for spiritual consultation and advice, preparing candidates for baptism, confirmation and reception, and instructing the children within their care in the Christian faith. Priests must provide such other ministrations as may be prescribed by law.

6. A priest may be admitted to such ecclesiastical office, if provided by law, as vicar general, archdeacon or dean, to which particular ministries attach.

Principle 34: Parish and other ministry

1. An ordained minister who has charge of a parish or other local ecclesiastical unit has the primary authority and responsibility for the care of souls therein.

2. An ordained minister may be authorised to assist in a parish or to function as a chaplain or in some other form of non-parochial ministry.

3. A minister exercises ministry under the general authority, oversight and pastoral direction of the diocesan bishop.

Principle 35: Admission to the order of bishops

1. Candidature for admission to the episcopate is reserved to priests who satisfy such requirements as to age, eligibility, suitability, learning, soundness of mind, good morals and such other prerequisites for the proper exercise of episcopal ministry as are prescribed by law.

2. A priest is admitted to the order of bishops by means of consecration.

3. Consecration of a bishop-elect shall not take place unless and until the appointment is confirmed by competent lawful authority.

4. Episcopal consecration shall not occur without the prior consent of the candidate.

5. Order is taken for episcopal consecration by the archbishop or principal bishop.

6. Consecration of a person as a bishop, consisting in the fulfilment of what the church universal intends, is effected, with the consent of the candidate, in accordance with the prescribed liturgical form through the laying on of hands by three validly consecrated bishops, the recital of the words of consecration and the invocation of the Holy Spirit to give grace for the work of a bishop.

Principle 36: Admission to the office of diocesan bishop

1. Election to the office of diocesan bishop is carried out by an electoral college or other such body, which may consist of representatives of the episcopate, clergy and laity.

2. An episcopal election may be challenged on substantive and procedural grounds by such persons, in such manner and to such extent as is provided by law.

3. The authority to confirm or reject the election of a bishop vests in an archbishop, episcopal assembly or other competent lawful authority.

4. Episcopal consecration is followed by inauguration of ministry in the diocese.

5. Enthronement or other installation in the diocese may follow confirmation in the case of a person already in episcopal orders.

Principle 37: Diocesan episcopal ministry

1. The diocesan bishop has a special responsibility and authority as the chief pastor, minister and teacher of the diocese and as a governor and guardian of discipline in the diocese, and exercises ministry in accordance with law.

2. The bishop as chief pastor must foster the spiritual welfare and unity of the diocese.

3. The bishop is the principal minister of the word and sacraments, with authority to ensure the worthiness of public worship, and has the right to preside at the eucharist, administer the sacraments, celebrate the rites of ordination and confirmation, preach the word and perform such other liturgical functions as are prescribed by law.

4. The bishop must teach, uphold and safeguard the faith and doctrine of the church.

5. The bishop has a role of leadership in the governance of the diocese, is president of the diocesan synod, council or equivalent assembly and performs such other governmental functions as may be prescribed by law.

6. The bishop has a primary responsibility to maintain ecclesiastical discipline in the diocese among clergy and laity in the manner and to the extent prescribed by law.

7. The diocesan bishop should reside in the diocese.

8. The ministry of a diocesan bishop terminates on vacancy of the see by the death, retirement, resignation or removal of that bishop in accordance with the law.

Principle 38: Episcopal assistance

1. A designated ecclesiastical authority may appoint a coadjutor bishop to the diocese, with a right of succession on vacancy, in such manner and to such extent as is authorised by law.

2. A diocesan bishop may have an assistant bishop, with no right of succession on a vacancy, with the approval of the authority designated by law for this purpose and subject to the satisfaction of such conditions as may be prescribed by law.

3. An assistant bishop may be commissioned or otherwise authorised by the diocesan bishop to undertake such ministry and perform such episcopal acts as may be lawfully required or permitted by that diocesan bishop.

4. An assistant bishop is subject to the ordinary jurisdiction of the diocesan bishop.

Principle 39: Archiepiscopal and metropolitical authority

1. The principal episcopal office in a province is that of archbishop, presiding bishop or moderator, an office to which metropolitical authority customarily attaches.

2. A person is assigned in a church to the principal episcopal office by election or other lawful process involving members of that church.

3. The principal bishop holds office for such term as may be prescribed by law.

4. Vacancy in the principal episcopal office occurs on death, resignation, completion of the term of office, retirement or removal as prescribed by law.

5. During the incapacity of a principal bishop, the functions of that office are to be carried out by such authority as is determined by law.

6. A principal bishop, in the manner and to the extent prescribed by law: exercises authority and leadership over the province; convenes and presides at its legislative and episcopal assemblies; oversees the episcopacy; exercises visitatorial and judicial functions assigned to that office; and represents the province in its external relations.

7. A principal bishop enjoys precedence over the bishops of the province to the extent authorised by law.

Principle 40: Primacy: the office of primate

1. An archbishop or bishop may be assigned to the office of primate or other such presiding episcopal office in a national, regional, provincial or other church.

2. A person is assigned in a church to the office of primate by election or other lawful process involving members of that church.

3. A primate is responsible for general leadership in initiating, developing and implementing the policy and strategy of a church.

4. A primate represents a church in its dealings with other churches, national and international bodies and has such other functions as are prescribed by law.

5. A primate exercises such jurisdiction as may be prescribed by law.

6. A primate is to hold office for such term as is prescribed by law.

Principle 41: Clerical discipleship

1. Clergy should fashion their ministry after the example of Jesus Christ.

2. Clergy should not act in any way or engage in any occupations, habits or recreations inconsistent with their sacred calling but should lead a disciplined way of life appropriate to their clerical state and office.

3. Clergy must be diligent in liturgical life, particularly in the celebration of the eucharist, and must apply themselves to personal prayer, self-examination and study, especially of Holy Scripture and other matters pertaining to ministerial duties.

4. Clergy must not engage in any secular employment or other occupation which affects their ministry without consultation with, or as the case may be permission from, the diocesan bishop or other relevant church authority.

5. Clergy should reside within the territorial boundaries of or near the ecclesiastical unit to which they are assigned; absence is permitted only with the consent of the diocesan bishop or other designated authority.

6. Clergy of the diocese are subject to the jurisdiction of the diocesan bishop to the extent provided under the law.

7. Clergy must comply with the lawful and honest directions of their diocesan bishop.

8. Clergy should dress in such manner (a) as is suitable to the performance of their ministry; and (b) as may be a sign and mark of their calling both to those within their charge and to society at large.

Principle 42: Authorised public ministry

1. Prior authorisation to exercise public ministry as an ordained or a lay person within a diocese must be obtained from the diocesan bishop or other designated authority.

2. The bishop may confer upon an ordained or a lay person the authority to minister publicly by means of appointment to a particular office or public ministry, by licence, by written permission or by such other process as may be prescribed by law.

3. The laity, or their representatives, participate in the appointment of clergy to an office or other public ministry in such manner, and to such extent, as may be prescribed by law.

4. Episcopal or other authorisation to exercise public ministry in a diocese may be refused for lawful reason.

5. No bishop, priest or deacon coming from another diocese, which includes a diocese in another church of the Anglican Communion, shall exercise public ministry in the host diocese without the prior permission of the host diocesan bishop.

6. Before they may be permitted by the bishop to minister in the diocese, clergy from another diocese, which includes a diocese in another church of the Anglican Communion, must produce to the host bishop such satisfactory evidence of ordination and good standing as may be lawfully required.

7. The withdrawal or termination of episcopal authority for any ordained or lay person to exercise public ministry in a diocese must be carried out in accordance with the grounds and procedures prescribed by law.

Principle 43: The professional ethic of public ministry

1. In all professional matters, ministers are to maintain practices that (a) give glory to God; (b) advance the goals, peace and unity of the church; (c) nurture and strengthen the welfare of fellow ministers, the faithful and the public; (d) demonstrate honest, fair and sincere motives; and (e) share faith, hope and love with all people.

2. Ministers should (a) recognise, affirm and protect the uniqueness and dignity of those to whom they minister irrespective of race, colour, ethnic or national origin, marital status, sex, sexual orientation, disability or age; and (b) respect the autonomy of those to whom they minister including their ultimate freedom to act contrary to the beliefs, practices and opinions of the minister.

3. Ministers are to act in such a manner as to (a) uphold and enhance the honour, integrity, morality, dignity, reputation and sacramentality of the ministry; and (b) maintain professional competency throughout their calling and limit their ministries to those activities and responsibilities for which they are duly qualified.

4. Ministers must ensure that no action or omission on their part or within their sphere of responsibility is detrimental to the well-being of another, and must not use their positions to further their own private interests or benefit.

5. Ministers must (a) behave at all times so as to deserve, retain and justify the trust and confidence of the church and of the public; and (b) deal with the affairs of the faithful and public sympathetically, effectively, promptly, rationally and without bias.

6. Ministers should be accountable to their church. They must not act arbitrarily but should give reasons for their decisions to those affected by them. They must be as open as possible in their dealings with fellow ministers, the faithful and the public, refusing to give information only when this is required by law or sufficient pastoral reasons weighed against the need for transparency.

7. Ministers must give accurate and truthful information at all times, correcting any inadvertent error at the earliest opportunity. They must not knowingly mislead any church authority, or any member of the faithful or of the public; nor should they seek to frustrate or otherwise obstruct synodical or any other lawful church process.

8. Ministry should be exercised in a nutritive and integrative way, never to exploit, manipulate or compete, but cultivating Christian virtues and fruits of the Spirit: love, joy, peace, patience, kindness, goodness, faithfulness, gentleness and self-control.

Principle 44: Pastoral care

1. Ministers offer their pastoral ministry, with respect and compassion, and without unlawful discrimination, not only to members of the congregation but to all people as witness to the example of Jesus the Good Shepherd.

2. Ministers, at all times and within reason, are (a) to be accessible and available for pastoral care; (b) to welcome those who visit them for pastoral care or other ministry and receive them as they would receive Christ; and (c) to act on requests from any person for a pastoral visit as promptly as is practicably possible.

3. Ministers should (a) encourage and enable the involvement of laypersons in pastoral work; and (b) acknowledge and act upon their own personal needs to receive ministry.

Principle 45: Professional and personal relationships

1. Ministers should (a) affirm and encourage the discipleship and ministry of all the faithful; (b) respect legitimate diversity of opinion and custom among the faithful; (c) promote collaborative ministry across church life and activity; and (d) foster vocations in order to assist people to discern and fulfil their own vocations.

2. Ministers must maintain appropriate professional boundaries at all times within the relationships encountered in the lawful exercise of ministry, including physical, sexual, emotional and psychological boundaries.

3. Ministers should be aware of and avoid possible risks of dependency, manipulation, competitiveness and collusion in professional relationships.

4. Ministers must display professional courtesy towards ministerial colleagues, must not initiate or engage in malicious talk about them and must respect confidences.

5. Ministers must be willing to serve with colleagues regardless of personal or theological differences unless otherwise permitted by lawful authority.

6. Ministers should respect the integrity of the ministry entrusted to others, in accordance with lawful authority.

7. Ministers should be understanding of the shortcomings of colleagues and seek to give support and help to them when needed. If ministers become aware of any inadequacy in themselves or in a colleague, the help of the wider church should be sought. Ministers, in the context of their own knowledge and experience, should assist fellow ministers to develop their own ministerial competence.

Principle 46: Confidentiality

1. All the faithful should respect confidences entrusted to them.

2. The acquisition, holding, processing and disclosure of confidential information within a church may be subject to rules of civil law.

3. Confidential information must not normally be disclosed unless this is required by civil law, consented to by the confider or necessary to prevent harm.

4. A person in ministry or office who engages in impermissible disclosure of confidential information received even outside sacramental confession may be subject to disciplinary process in the manner and to the extent provided by church law.

Principle 47: Termination of clerical ministry

1. Clergy may tender a resignation to the bishop and must resign or may be removed if their incapacity or unfitness to discharge ministry is lawfully established.

2. Clergy must retire from the offices they hold at such age as may be fixed by law but may continue in public ministry with the approval of the bishop or other competent authority in the manner and to the extent prescribed by law.

3. A person may voluntarily relinquish the exercise of holy orders. Relinquishment may be reversed in such circumstances as may be allowed under the law.

4. A person may be deposed from holy orders by lawful pronouncement of a competent ecclesiastical authority.

5. Deposition disables the exercise of holy orders, either irreversibly or reversibly, as the case may be, according to the law.

Part V: Doctrine and Liturgy

This section addresses the issues of doctrine and liturgy. In the Anglican tradition, neither doctrine nor liturgy is 'free-floating'. Each is bound by authority, doctrine being derived from Scripture and affirmed by the Catholic creeds and historic Anglican formularies; and liturgy has Scripture and the historic deposit of the Book of Common Prayer 1662 as its touchstones.

In each case, there are particular but overlapping roles for bishops, clergy and laity. All are called in their distinctive roles, to guard, teach, proclaim and live out this faith, in ways which are loyal to all that has been received from the past but which do justice to 'local circumstances, practices and needs'.

Through it all runs the certainty that in Christ, God's revelation is made known, controlling the church's faith, commanding the worship of the faithful and energising the whole body 'to illuminate, challenge and transform cultures, structures, thinking and doing'.

Principle 48: The presentation of doctrine

1. Doctrine is the teaching of the church on any matter of faith which a church receives, believes and represents afresh from generation to generation by virtue of its belonging to the One, Holy, Catholic and Apostolic Church.

2. The faithful have a responsibility to proclaim the Word of God revealed in Christ.

3. Bishops have a special responsibility to teach the faith, to state publicly the doctrine of the church and to expound their application to the people and issues of the age.

4. Priests and deacons have a responsibility to preach sermons and provide other forms of instruction in the faith for those entrusted to their charge.

5. Sermons may be preached, and instruction in the faith provided, by such laypersons as have received lawful authority to exercise a teaching ministry.

6. In sermons or other forms of teaching a minister must endeavour with care and sincerity to expound the word of truth according to Holy Scripture, to the glory of God and to the edification of the people.

7. A sermon should be preached at least on Sundays.

8. Clergy must take care that those in their care, especially children and young persons, are instructed in the doctrine, sacraments and discipline of Christ, as the Lord has commanded and as found in Holy Scripture, and in the teaching and catechism of a church.

9. A church may have commissions, boards, councils or other such bodies to lead, advise on and carry out the work of evangelism, mission and teaching at the appropriate levels of and in a manner prescribed by that church.

Principle 49: The sources of doctrine

1. The faith of our Lord Jesus Christ is taught in the Holy Scriptures, summed up in the Creeds and affirmed by the ancient Fathers and undisputed General Councils.

2. The Holy Scriptures of the Old and New Testaments contain all things necessary to salvation and are the rule and ultimate standard of faith.

3. The Apostles' Creed represents the baptismal symbol; and the Nicene Creed is recognised as the sufficient statement of the Christian faith.

4. The Thirty-Nine Articles of Religion, the Book of Common Prayer and the Ordinal 1662 are grounded in the Holy Scriptures, and in such teachings of the ancient Fathers and Councils of the Church as are agreeable to the Holy Scriptures.

5. The Thirty-Nine Articles of Religion, the Book of Common Prayer and the Ordinal 1662 as locally adapted represent historic sources or statements of lawful doctrine for a church.

Principle 50: The development of doctrinal formularies

1. A church must maintain the faith, doctrine, sacraments and discipline of the One, Holy, Catholic and Apostolic Church, and its own doctrinal formularies shall be compatible with the faith revealed in Holy Scripture,

summed up in the Creeds and received, practised and held by the church universal in the light of tradition and reason.

2. A church may draw up its own formularies of faith set out in terms that it considers suitable to the present day and to the needs of its people and circumstances so that the faith may be presented loyally and intelligibly from generation to generation.

3. Such competence as there may be to develop, reformulate or alter doctrinal formulas vests only in national, regional or provincial assemblies within a church according to its law.

4. The development of doctrinal formulas by a church assembly may be subject to such substantive limitations and special procedural requirements as may be prescribed by the law of a church to ensure the protection of the faith of the church universal.

5. A church may have a doctrinal commission or similar body to advise on and propose doctrinal development to the extent and in the manner prescribed by law.

Principle 51: Preaching, teaching and outreach

1. Ministry involves the proclamation of the gospel and instruction of the people in the faith. Ministers should lead people to greater exploration and fuller understanding of the gospel and its challenge to contemporary life within the tradition of faith.

2. Ministers are to ensure that biblical texts are treated respectfully and coherently, building on tradition and scholarship, so that scriptural revelation may continue to illuminate, challenge and transform cultures, structures, thinking and doing.

3. Ministers should bring new insights and knowledge to the interpretation and application of Scripture, so that the gospel can be proclaimed to this age as the good news that it has been to ages past.

4. Responsibility for mission in any place belongs primarily to a church in that place.

Principle 52: Legitimate theological diversity

1. Ministers are called to work together and remain in fellowship so that visible communion is maintained even if theological or other disagreements occur.

2. The right to deny the authenticity of the ministry of anyone duly authorised by a church belongs only to the competent ecclesiastical authority as designated by law.

3. A minister enjoys such rights of conscientious objection with impunity as are permitted by law.

Principle 53: Doctrinal discipline

1. The church has authority in controversies of faith.

2. At ordination and consecration candidates must subscribe to, assent to or otherwise affirm publicly their belief in or loyalty to the doctrine of their church.

3. Ordained ministers may be required to subscribe to the doctrine of their church on admission to an office or other appointment.

4. Lay ministers or lay officers may be required to subscribe to the doctrine of their church to the extent prescribed by law.

5. The width of permissible theological opinion in a church is determined, as the case may be under its law, (a) legislatively, by its central assembly; (b) executively, by its bishops, individually or collectively; and (c) judicially, by its courts and tribunals.

6. The bishop has a special responsibility to guard and uphold sound and wholesome doctrine.

7. Ministers must not teach, preach, publish or profess doctrine or belief incompatible with that of their own church.

8. A person who engages in unlawful doctrinal dissent may be subject to disciplinary process in church courts or tribunals in the manner and to the extent provided by law.

9. The courts and tribunals of a church do not declare true doctrine or create new doctrine but only state what the law is with regard to doctrine.

10. The interpretation of the standards and formularies of, and all questions of faith and doctrine arising in, a church shall be determined within that church save to the extent that its law permits reference for the purpose of consultation or determination of such matters to a body external to that church.

Principle 54: Liturgy and public worship

1. The worship of God is a fundamental action and responsibility of the church.

2. Worship of God involves praise, adoration, confession, prayer and thanksgiving.

3. Liturgy is the work of the faithful through corporate public worship in accordance with the lawful forms of service of a church.

4. A balance should be struck between preservation of the liturgical inheritance and adaptations to local use and the needs of the people and the age.

5. Rubrics and other norms in a service book provide for order and decorum in liturgy, enable the community to participate fully in the act of worship and ensure adaptability to meet local circumstances, practices and needs.

6. Regular attendance at corporate public worship is a fundamental duty of the faithful.

7. All the faithful should celebrate and keep the Lord`s Day, commonly called Sunday, by regular participation in corporate public worship, by hearing the Word of God read and taught, by acts of devotion and of charity, using all godly and sober conversation, and by abstention from all unnecessary labour and business.

8. Forms of service must be in a language understood by the people.

9. Local customs may be followed in the matter of posture, whether of standing, kneeling or sitting, at the time of public worship.

10. All persons present should pay reverent attention at the time of divine worship, give due reverence to the name of the Lord Jesus and stand at the Creed and the reading of the Gospel at the Holy Communion.

11. The officiating minister is responsible for music at public worship, should collaborate in this matter with the congregation, organist, choirmaster or other director of music, and should take account of local custom.

12. Chants, hymns, anthems and other settings must be appropriate, in both words and music, to the acts of worship and prayer as well as to the congregation, and must not be contrary to church doctrine but glorify God and help the people in worship.

13. Disagreements about music may be referred to the bishop for resolution.

14. Ministers should wear at the time of divine service such vesture as is the customary ecclesiastical apparel of their order or office, and questions of vesture, its introduction or its disuse should be determined by the bishop according to law.

Principle 55: Liturgical revision: the forms of service

1. The normative authority of the Book of Common Prayer 1662 for the liturgical regime of a church is such as may be recognised by the history and law of that church.

2. A church may make such revisions, adaptations and innovations in the forms of service, lectionary and calendar as are desirable to adapt to particular needs and circumstances.

3. A church may have a commission or other body to prepare, advise on and recommend liturgical adaptation and innovation.

4. Authority over the approval, amendment, continuance or discontinuance of forms of service vests in the central church assembly to the extent and in the manner prescribed by law.

5. A form of service must be such as is neither contrary to, nor indicative of a departure from, the doctrine of the church in any essential matter.

6. Liturgical adaptation and innovation must be consistent with the Word of God and, to the extent provided by the law of a church, with the spirit and teaching of the Book of Common Prayer 1662 or other recognised historic formularies.

7. It is for the central church assembly, or other ecclesiastical body authorised by it, to approve, in such manner and to such extent as is provided by law, new forms of service for experimental use, during such period and subject to such conditions as may be prescribed by law, which use in a diocese may be authorised by its bishop.

8. The bishop may authorise for a diocese variations of, adjustments to, substitutes for or additions to any part of a liturgical text under trial use to the extent permitted by law.

9. If permitted by law, a bishop or other ecclesiastical body may authorise services for use in a diocese, for which no provision already exists, subject

to such limits as are imposed by law, and provided such services are not inconsistent with church doctrine.

10. No minister in a parish or other local unit may formulate or use a form of service for which no provision exists in authorised service books without lawful authority.

Principle 56: Liturgical administration

1. A minister must use in public worship only those forms of service authorised or otherwise permitted by lawful authority.

2. A church may require uniformity of a single liturgical use throughout that church or conformity with a number of alternative services.

3. Liturgical life should be characterised by flexibility to the extent authorised by law.

4. Appropriate patterns of worship may vary from place to place and from time to time, and if authorised to do so, ministers may use their own sensitivity and discretion to conduct worship so the faithful may participate with sincerity and understanding.

5. A minister may make and use variations in an authorised form of service in the manner and to the extent prescribed by law, and such variations must be reverent and seemly and not be contrary to or a departure from the doctrine of the church.

6. Rubrics or other liturgical directions are to be interpreted and applied flexibly so as to enable adaptation to meet local circumstances, practices and needs.

7. The diocesan bishop has a special responsibility and authority to oversee and control liturgical practice in the diocese in accordance with law.

8. Questions concerning liturgical variation by a minister may be referred to the bishop, who may give such permission or pastoral guidance, advice or direction as is deemed appropriate in such manner and to such extent as is prescribed by law.

9. Failure by a minister to use the authorised forms of service or otherwise to conduct public worship in accordance with the law may result in disciplinary action.

Principle 57: The provision of public worship

1. In each parish there should be a place of worship in which the clergy duly appointed regularly conduct public worship, administer the sacraments and perform other ecclesiastical rites and ceremonies with the participation of the laity.

2. Clergy should make provision for public worship, and lead the worship of the congregations committed to their charge, unless hindered by sickness or other reasonable cause approved by lawful authority.

3. Public worship may be dispensed with in times of necessity for reasonable cause on an occasional or a regular basis if so authorised by the minister, parish assembly, bishop or other lawful authority to the extent permitted by law.

4. A minister should prepare services of worship thoughtfully, carefully and collaboratively, with consideration for the needs of the locality and people, especially disabled or disadvantaged members of the congregation.

Principle 58: Liturgical choice: alternative forms of service

1. The choice between any alternative authorised forms of service rests, as the case may be, either with the minister alone or acting in collaboration with the parish assembly, or with such other authority as is designated by law.

2. The choice of forms of service for occasional offices, such as baptisms, marriages and funerals, lies with the officiating minister, who should consult the parties concerned.

3. Disagreements over the choice of alternative forms of service, including those for occasional offices, may be referred to the bishop for advice or determination.

Principle 59: Responsible public worship

1. Clergy should share liturgical functions with those authorised to perform them, encourage the faithful to participate fully and in roles of leadership in liturgy, and provide for training and preparation as necessary to support them.

2. The right to supervise the conduct of public worship in a parish or other local unit vests in the member of clergy or other authorised person responsible for that parish.

3. No minister, lay or ordained, from another parish or diocese may officiate or conduct divine services publicly in whole or in part within a parish or other local unit without the prior consent of its member of clergy or other person authorised by law.

4. The oversight of public worship in the diocese is subject to the general direction of the bishop or other designated lawful authority.

Principle 60: Liturgical discipline

1. The bishop has authority to oversee liturgy and public worship within the diocese.

2. The bishop or other designated authority is competent to restrain or prohibit in the conduct of liturgy and public worship any significant practice or grave irregularity not provided for in service books or permitted by other lawful authority.

3. Church members should submit themselves, in all matters ritual and ceremonial, to the authoritative judgments of their church.

4. Ministers must in the administration of liturgy and public worship comply with church discipline and observe the forms of service authorised for use in their church, so as to ensure a reverent, regular and careful ordering of divine worship.

5. Disputes concerning liturgy and public worship shall be determined within a church save to the extent that its law permits reference for the purpose of consultation or determination of such matters to a body external to that church.

6. Any minister who fails to provide public worship, to administer the sacraments or to use lawful liturgical ritual or ceremonial, according to the order and use of a church, may be the subject of disciplinary proceedings in its courts or tribunals.

Part VI: Ecclesiastical Rites

This section deals with the two key dominical sacraments of baptism and the eucharist, and goes on to cover marriage issues, confession and absolution, exorcism and funeral rites.

Perhaps unsurprisingly within a worldwide Communion whose liturgical life was essentially shaped by the Church of England Book of Common Prayer (1662), there has been widespread agreement over matters of form, including agreement about the principles of liturgical revision in individual churches. At the same time, historic tensions between the Catholic and Protestant emphases within Anglicanism are never far from the surface.

From the lawyer's point of view, marriage law presents a particularly interesting study in the overlap between church law and the law of the state. The interplay between the exercise of civil legal rights in relation to divorce and remarriage on the one hand and the teaching of the churches on the other has resulted in the development of very diverse approaches to these issues within the churches of the Anglican Communion.

The working groups operating under the auspices of the Ecclesiastical Law Society, as part of the revision process worldwide for this second iteration of the Principles, *reported significant changes in some church laws with regard to whether two persons of the same sex may marry. As a result, there are now differences between the laws of the churches of the Communion on this point. Some churches provide only for marriage between one man and one woman. Some churches also provide for marriage between people of the same sex. Mindful of this difference, and of the principle of autonomy, it has not been possible to discern a common principle of canon law on who may marry whom.*

Moreover, a distinction should be drawn between canon law and civil law with regard to marriage, divorce and nullity. While the church may operate within the civil law with respect to marriage, divorce and nullity, canon law and civil law may differ. These principles are concerned with canon law and, to the extent it may be relevant, the interaction with civil law.

The revision process has also demonstrated changes in relation to the seal of the confessional, particularly as a result of developments concerning the safeguarding of children and vulnerable adults. It is in turn important to note that the seal of the confessional must be distinguished from rules of confidentiality in civil law.

Principle 61: Baptism: nature and administration

1. The sacrament of baptism, instituted by Christ, is a sign of regeneration or new birth by which those who receive it are incorporated into the church of Christ.

2. A valid baptism is administered with water, by way of pouring, sprinkling, immersion, submersion or other similar means, simultaneously with the form of words 'I baptise you in the name of the Father and of the Son and of the Holy Spirit.'

3. All baptised persons belong to the church universal.

4. Baptism alone may not effect institutional membership of a church save to the extent provided by its law.

5. Baptism by a priest is the norm. Baptism may be administered by a deacon to the extent provided by law.

6. Baptism may be administered by a layperson in cases of emergency such as danger of death.

7. Baptism should be administered publicly in the presence of the congregation at the regular church services.

8. Baptism may be administered privately to the extent permitted by law.

9. Baptisms must be recorded in a register maintained especially for this purpose.

10. Valid baptism is indelible and cannot be repeated.

Principle 62: Sponsorship and baptismal instruction

1. The number of godparents or other sponsors for baptismal candidates is customarily two or such other number as may be prescribed by law.

2. At least one godparent or other sponsor should be of the same sex as the candidate, and godparents or other sponsors shall be of such age as may be prescribed by law.

3. Parents or guardians of a candidate may function as sponsors, and the law may recommend that one of the sponsors be a parent of that candidate.

4. Subject to such dispensations as may be permitted by law, godparents or other sponsors must be baptised persons and should be communicants.

5. Godparents or other sponsors have the responsibility to help the baptised person grow in the knowledge and love of God and in the fellowship of the church, and support such person by prayer and example of Christian living.

6. Parents, guardians, godparents or other sponsors of infant candidates are to receive instruction or other preparation prior to the baptism, by persons lawfully designated, as to the sacrament itself and the Christian life entered by it.

7. Prior to baptism the minister is to instruct and prepare, or cause to be instructed and prepared, any adult, or other candidate able to answer for themselves, in the Christian faith, the meaning and significance of baptism and the Christian life entered by it.

Principle 63: Baptismal discipline: admission and exclusion

1. Parents or guardians are expected to bring their children to baptism.

2. No minister may without lawful cause refuse or unduly delay baptism of a child in their cure whose parents or guardians desire baptism for the child.

3. In the exercise of pastoral and moral responsibility, a minister may, after due notice, postpone baptism until the parents or guardians and godparents or other sponsors have been instructed and are in the opinion of that minister in a position to undertake the spiritual, moral and educational obligations required of them.

4. A minister should not baptise a child without the consent of its parents or guardians.

5. Adult candidates for baptism must satisfy the requirements of faith, repentance and such other conditions as may be prescribed under the law.

6. When adults are to be baptised, they should be presented to the bishop for confirmation either at the same time or as soon as possible thereafter.

7. If a minister refuses or unduly delays the baptism of any child, the parents or guardians may apply to the bishop, who shall, after consultation with the minister, give such directions as are deemed appropriate.

8. A minister who refuses to baptise without lawful cause may be subject to disciplinary process for neglect of duty in accordance with law.

Principle 64: Conditional baptism

1. Due to the indelibility of baptism, the minister of baptism must be satisfied that a candidate for baptism has not previously been baptised.

2. If there is uncertainty or other reasonable doubt as to whether a candidate has been baptised previously, such person may be baptised conditionally.

3. Conditional baptism must be administered as no mere formality but with the solemnity proper to a rite of Christian initiation.

4. The absence of a baptismal certificate or other record is not in itself sufficient reason for conditional baptism.

Principle 65: Confirmation

1. Only a baptised person who has attained the age of discretion may be confirmed.

2. Confirmation is a rite in which a person makes a profession of the faith and a mature expression or reaffirmation of the commitment to Christ made at baptism.

3. The minister of confirmation is the bishop.

4. Confirmation is effected by episcopal laying on of hands and invocation of the Holy Spirit to strengthen the candidate in the Christian life.

5. Confirmation may be administered at a celebration of the eucharist.

6. The duty to encourage a person to be confirmed rests upon the baptismal sponsors and sometimes with or in collaboration with the parents or guardians.

7. A special duty to seek out candidates for confirmation may be placed on clergy.

8. An ordained minister presents candidates to the bishop for confirmation, which should be witnessed and recorded in a certificate or other document.

9. All confirmation candidates must receive instruction, from an ordained minister or other authorised person, in the Christian faith, which may include the Lord's Prayer, the Apostles' Creed, the Ten Commandments and church catechism, so that candidates may render an account of their faith and the bishop may be assured by the presenting minister of their faith, repentance and resolve to live the Christian life.

10. In cases of the baptism of adults and of children able to answer for themselves, baptism and confirmation should be administered as a single rite, failing which confirmation should follow baptism as soon as is convenient.

Principle 66: Holy Communion: nature and celebration

1. Holy Communion, the eucharist or the Lord's Supper, is a sacrament instituted by Christ, the central act of worship and an act of the whole church, and shall be maintained and duly administered by each church.

2. Every confirmed person should receive Holy Communion regularly.

3. Holy Communion should be administered in a church building or other place of worship, except for the communion of the sick or the housebound, or in other cases with the permission of the bishop or other lawful authority.

4. The authorised forms of service must be used to celebrate Holy Communion.

5. The elements to be consecrated for Holy Communion are bread and wine.

6. The giving of Holy Communion in both kinds is the normal practice, according to the example and precept of our Lord.

7. Presidency at the Holy Communion is reserved to a bishop or priest.

8. It is the prerogative of the bishop, when present, to be the principal celebrant at the Holy Communion.

9. A deacon, or a lay minister specially authorised by the bishop as a eucharistic assistant, may assist in the distribution of the Holy Communion.

Principle 67: Reservation of the sacrament

1. The sacrament may be reserved for the sick and housebound, for those dying or in special need and for devotional services, with the lawful permission of the bishop.

2. The reserved sacrament must be kept in a safe and fitting place in a church building.

Principle 68: Admission to Holy Communion

1. To receive Holy Communion, a person must be baptised and, where required by the law of a church, confirmed or ready and desirous to be confirmed.

2. Where confirmation remains a requirement for admission to Holy Communion, a bishop may authorise such admission of baptised and unconfirmed persons to the extent lawfully permitted.

Principle 69: Exclusion from Holy Communion

1. No minister shall without lawful cause deny Holy Communion to any baptised Christian who devoutly and humbly desires it.

2. A church may make provision in its general law for persons, in the absence of repentance and amendment of life, to be excluded from Holy Communion for living openly in grievous sin or contention, causing scandal to the congregation, bringing the church into disrepute or similar causes prescribed by law.

3. A priest may summarily exclude a person from Holy Communion to prevent immediate scandal in church and must take steps to report the matter to the bishop, who after due investigation must issue appropriate directions with which the priest shall comply.

4. In cases other than summary exclusion, if a priest is empowered by law to exclude a person from Holy Communion, such priest must first warn the person not to receive and may exclude that person only if there is no repentance and amendment of life.

5. If a priest warns a person not to receive Holy Communion, and the warning is unheeded, the priest must refer the matter to the bishop, who may exclude that person if so authorised by law.

6. A person excluded from Holy Communion may appeal (a) against exclusion by a priest, to the bishop, or (b) if provided by law, against exclusion by or a direction of the bishop, to an episcopal assembly, court or other competent authority.

7. In appeals against exclusion from Holy Communion the competent authority must after due investigation issue appropriate directions, which shall be complied with.

8. Restoration to admission to Holy Communion is reserved to the bishop or priest, as the case may be under church law, or in cases of appeal to the competent authority.

9. The effects of exclusion from Holy Communion are such as may be prescribed by law.

Principle 70: Marriage: nature, purposes and responsibilities

As stated in the preamble to Part VI, the working groups operating under the auspices of the Ecclesiastical Law Society, as part of the revision process worldwide for this second iteration of the principles, reported significant changes in some church laws with regard to whether two persons of the same sex may marry. As a result, there are now differences between the laws of the churches of the Communion on this point. Some churches provide only for marriage between one man and one woman. Some churches also provide for marriage between people of the same sex.

Mindful of this difference, and of the principle of autonomy, it has not been possible to discern a common principle of canon law on who may marry whom.

Unlike the other 2022 revisions, which proceeded by consensus, the revision committee decided the method to record this development by majority vote.

Principle 70 as agreed in 2008 is included below for information.

1. Marriage, an honourable estate instituted by God, is an exclusive life-long union, signifying the mystical union that is between Christ and his Church, effected on the free exchange of consents between one man and one woman joined together by God as husband and wife and lasting until the death of one spouse.

2. Marriage is a creative relationship between a husband and a wife to share life together in the spirit of Jesus Christ for the development of their personalities, for the procreation and nurture of children, to direct the right use of the natural instincts and affections, and for the mutual society, help and comfort which the one ought to have for the other, both in prosperity and adversity, and for the establishment of a home and family life.

3. All members of a church share according to their circumstances in the obligation to uphold Christian standards of marriage in human society especially by care for their own families and by neighbourly care for the families of others.

Principle 71: Requirements for ecclesiastical marriage

1. Ministers must comply with civil law as to the formation of marriage and with church law as to the solemnisation of marriage according to ecclesiastical rites.

2. The parties to a marriage must satisfy the civil and ecclesiastical requirements for a valid marriage. Otherwise the minister should refuse solemnisation.

3. An ecclesiastical marriage is presumed valid if: (a) the parties have a right under civil law to contract a marriage; (b) both parties freely and knowingly consent to marry, without fraud, coercion or mistake as to the identity of a partner or the mental condition of the other party; (c) the parties do not fall within the prohibited degrees of relationship; (d) the parties have attained the required age for marriage; and (e) where required in the case of minors, their parents or guardians have consented to it.

4. A church is free to impose for spiritual purposes such conditions for admission to ecclesiastical marriage as are prescribed by its law.

5. While a Christian marriage is one between baptised persons, the law may provide for marriage where the normal requirement of baptism is not met.

6. A church may relax baptismal requirements for marriage by way of dispensation or permission of a bishop or other competent authority to the extent prescribed by law.

7. A person, being a member of, associated with or resident in a parish of, a church, is entitled to solemnisation of marriage in accordance with the rites of that church in the manner and to the extent provided by its law.

8. A minister may refuse to solemnise a marriage for such cause, which may include conscientious objection, as is provided by the law.

Principle 72: Preliminaries for ecclesiastical marriage

1. A minister should instruct prospective spouses in the nature, significance, purpose and responsibilities of marriage in a manner consistent with church doctrine.

2. The precise content of marriage preparation and its duration may be determined by the minister, the bishop or other competent ecclesiastical authority.

3. Such notice of the proposed date of the marriage as may be prescribed by law must be given to the relevant minister, unless dispensed with for lawful cause.

4. Preliminaries to the solemnisation of marriage in church may include the publication of banns, the issuing of an episcopal licence or other lawful procedure carried out by a designated authority and compliance with any additional civil law requirements.

5. Before marriage is solemnised it must be established that no impediment obstructs its valid celebration.

6. If any impediment is alleged, marriage should be deferred until the truth is established.

Principle 73: Solemnisation of marriage

1. The ordinary minister of holy matrimony is a priest or bishop, but the parties may also be understood as both the recipients and the ministers of marriage.

2. A deacon may conduct a marriage service to such extent as may be provided in the law of the church and the civil law.

3. The choice of marriage service, if alternatives are provided by a church, belongs to the minister who conducts the service in consultation with the parties concerned.

4. A marriage is created by the free, competent and open consent of the parties who contract it, in the presence of witnesses and of an authorised minister.

5. A marriage must be witnessed by at least two persons and recorded in registers or other resources provided and maintained for this purpose by a designated authority.

6. A church may provide for the blessing of a civil marriage.

Principle 74: Nullity of marriage

1. A church may provide that any person whose marriage has been terminated by divorce or annulment under civil law may apply, in the manner prescribed by church law, to the bishop or other competent ecclesiastical authority for a judgment which may declare the nullity of the marriage for ecclesiastical purposes.

2. To the extent that a church may so provide, grounds for an ecclesiastical declaration of nullity may include: absence of consent freely given and received, or of an intention to be married until death; lack of the required age to marry; or being within the prohibited degrees of relationship.

3. Marriage in church may follow a declaration of nullity of a former marriage.

Principle 75: Divorce and remarriage in church

1. The parties to marriage are required to declare their intention that their matrimonial bond be dissolved only by the death of one of them.

2. When a marriage is dissolved by the death of one of the parties, the surviving spouse is free to marry in church.

3. A church may provide that, when marital unity is imperilled, before recourse to civil law, the spouses should approach the church, which should labour that the parties may be reconciled.

4. If the situation between spouses has become such that a harmonious or even tolerable relationship has in fact ceased to exist, a church may hold that while divorce is undesirable it may be preferable to the continuance of a destructive relationship.

5. Remarriage after a civil dissolution may be permitted in accordance with the requirements of a church.

6. An ordained minister may refuse for reasons of conscience or other lawful cause to solemnise the marriage of a divorced person whose former spouse is still alive.

7. A church may provide that the decision to solemnise the marriage of a divorced person whose former spouse still lives is to be made by a member of the clergy, as the case may be, either alone, or in consultation with the bishop, or with the consent of the bishop or such other competent authority prescribed by law.

8. A person who has obtained a civil divorce should not by virtue of that fact alone be excluded from Holy Communion.

9. Persons who remarry during the lifetime of a former spouse and those married to them may receive Holy Communion subject to conditions operative under the law.

Principle 76: Confession and absolution

1. Only a priest or bishop may pronounce absolution.

2. Priests and bishops may exercise the ministry of general confession and absolution at a public service, and private confession and absolution to an individual person.

3. Priests should instruct the faithful in the use of private confession.

4. A person who, unable to quiet their conscience by general confession or otherwise to find the assurance of the forgiveness of God, repents of their sinful past and intends amendment of life may offer private confession to God in the presence of a priest.

5. At a private confession the priest may give advice and must pronounce absolution except for good reason.

6. The normal minister of private confession is the priest having cure of souls of the parish in which it is performed.

Principle 77: The seal of the confessional

1. The seal of the confessional is inviolable save when the law of the church expressly provides for disclosure despite the seal.

2. The extent to which the seal of the confessional is protected and priest-penitent communications are privileged in civil courts is a matter of civil law.

3. A priest who violates the seal of the confessional may be subject to judicial or other disciplinary proceedings carried out in accordance with church law.

Principle 78: Deliverance or exorcism

1. The ministry of deliverance is reserved to the bishop or those whom the bishop appoints.

2. All persons who exercise the ministry of deliverance should do so with great care to ensure that they act only with the knowledge and authority of the bishop.

3. The ministry of deliverance should be followed by appropriate pastoral care.

Principle 79: Death and burial rites

1. To prepare a person for death a church may offer anointing or imposition of hands.

2. Disposal of a body after death must be reverent and may be by burial, cremation or other lawful process, or a combination of these.

3. No minister may without lawful cause refuse or delay disposal, in accordance with the funeral rites of a church, of the remains of any person brought to the designated place.

4. The administration of funeral rites for those who die unbaptised, those who take their own lives and such others as may be prescribed by law may be subject to direction from or consultation with the diocesan bishop.

5. The minister of funeral rites is normally a person in holy orders. Lay ministers also may conduct funerals to the extent authorised by law.

6. The choice of funeral rites, if alternatives are authorised, belongs to the officiating minister in consultation with or with the consent of the family or friends of the deceased.

7. The remains of a Christian should be disposed of in a consecrated place or, if the place is not consecrated, in a place which has been blessed.

Part VII: Church Property

This section addresses a wide variety of issues relating to the ownership, use, and care of church property, real and personal, by ecclesiastical authorities at all levels of a church. The recurrent theme is the church's interest in ensuring that property be set aside, used and maintained with reverence and integrity to further the mission of the church. These responsibilities apply equally to space consecrated for worship, land used for church programmes, parish furnishings and records, and monetary and other contributions made to support the clergy and otherwise carry out church functions.

While day-to-day management of church property should be left to appropriate local church entities, their responsibilities may be prescribed by law adopted at other levels of authority, so that persons entrusted with the care of church property are held accountable for preserving it 'for the mission of a church, and for the benefit and the use of its members, from generation to generation, in accordance with the law of that church'.

Stewardship responsibilities regarding church property include provision for support of the parish through offerings from its members, contributions to the work of the diocese and the national assembly, and protection of church property through diligent maintenance, sound investment and adequate insurance.

Provision should be made by the law of a church for the use of church funds to support the clergy and their families through stipends, provision for housing, and medical, disability and retirement plans.

The highest standards of integrity in handling church funds are required of both clergy and laity.

Principle 80: Ownership and administration of church property

1. Churches should satisfy those requirements of civil law which apply to the acquisition, ownership, administration and alienation of church property, both real and personal.

2. Property is held by those authorities within a church which have legal personality as trustees or other entities of a fiduciary nature under civil law and competence under church law.

3. Ecclesiastical authorities are the stewards of church property.

4. Ecclesiastical authorities must hold and administer church property to advance the mission of a church, and for the benefit and use of its members, from generation to generation, in accordance with the law of that church.

5. Church property is held in trust for a church and should not be alienated or encumbered without such consents as may be prescribed by law.

6. Ecclesiastical trustees may sell, purchase and exchange property in the manner and to the extent authorised by law.

7. The central assembly of a church, or other designated assembly, may frame laws for the management and use of property held in trust for that church.

8. Commissions, boards and other bodies may be appointed to advise church trustees on the development and administration of any property held by those trustees.

9. The management and day-to-day administration of church property at the local level are vested in parish assemblies or other legal entities and are subject to such prerogatives of the clergy as may be provided by law.

10. National, regional, provincial, diocesan, parish or other church trustees must perform their functions under the order and control of the appropriate assembly to which the law of a church renders them accountable.

11. No one shall deny or obstruct access to any ecclesiastical person or body lawfully entitled to enter or use church property.

Principle 81: Consecration and care of places of worship

1. Buildings may be designated by lawful authority as places of public worship.

2. Places of public worship and for Christian burial may be set aside for the purposes of God by consecration or dedication.

3. The consecration, dedication or other act which sets aside property for the purposes of God is customarily performed by a bishop.

4. Effects of consecration or dedication of property may be removed by a bishop or other ecclesiastical authority in the manner and to the extent permitted by law.

5. Consecrated or dedicated church property may not be used for purposes inconsistent with the uses of God for which it is set aside.

6. Wardens or other stewards must not allow churches to be profaned by any temporal use inconsistent with the sanctity of the place and sound doctrine.

7. The day-to-day control, direction and administration of places of worship vest in the parish council or other local assembly, which, subject to the jurisdiction of national, provincial or diocesan bodies, shall cause all proper and reasonable care to be taken of them and their furniture and ornaments, and endeavour to keep them decent, clean and in good repair.

8. Episcopal or other lawful consent, whether executive or judicial, must be obtained for any alteration or addition to or removal of property from places of worship to such extent and in such manner, and subject to such appeals, as may be prescribed by law.

9. An inventory should be kept of the contents of places of worship, and may be subject to inspection at prescribed times by a competent ecclesiastical authority.

10. A competent ecclesiastical authority should inspect places of worship and their contents at such regular intervals as may be prescribed by law.

Principle 82: Residential accommodation for clergy

1. The law of a church may require that provision be made for clergy to have appropriate accommodation.

2. Where a residence is provided by a church, responsibility for care and maintenance of that residence is shared by occupying clergy and that church in the manner and to the extent fixed by law.

3. Where a residence is provided by a church, the diocese should carry out periodic inspections of that residence in the manner and to the extent provided by church law.

4. Where a residence is provided by a church, the occupation of that residence may be terminated or otherwise restricted only in the manner and to the extent provided by law.

Principle 83: Ecclesiastical registers and records

1. In each parish or other local unit there must be kept such registers or records of services, baptisms, confirmations, marriages, burials and funerals, communicants and church members as may be required by law.

2. The safe custody of ecclesiastical registers and records is the duty of the minister and wardens acting individually, or jointly, or together with the local parish assembly.

3. To ensure they are updated and maintained, registers and records should be inspected regularly by competent ecclesiastical authority.

4. Ecclesiastical registers and records should be subject to reasonable access.

5. A church may provide for the collection, maintenance and preservation of ecclesiastical documents of permanent value.

6. Each church must administer its archives, ensure ready access and encourage diocesan authorities to have a proper care for diocesan and parochial archives either in secure conditions within their own offices, or

in recognised regional archival repositories available for historical research and other purposes.

Principle 84: Financial stewardship

1. A church should be financially self-supporting.

2. Each unit within a church should be entrusted with a share in the responsibilities for, and control and direction of, the finances in that church.

3. An ecclesiastical organisation must comply with such financial procedures and controls as are prescribed by law.

4. An ecclesiastical organisation must keep financial accounts and submit an annual report with the audited accounts to the appropriate church assembly in order for that assembly to review the financial management and affairs of that organisation.

Principle 85: Financial propriety in ministry

1. A minister should ensure the highest standards, of honesty, integrity, openness and care, in both professional and personal financial activities.

2. A minister must keep separate church and personal finances to avoid any possibility of suspicion or impropriety, fraud or deception.

3. Ministers should not inappropriately or unlawfully ask for or make use of the money, possessions or other property of any person to whom they minister.

4. Financial remuneration is not the object of ministry, and ministers must (a) not receive any unauthorised advantage from the exercise of ministry; (b) refuse any gift, favour or hospitality that might be interpreted, now or in the future, as an attempt to obtain preferential consideration or treatment; and (c) not require or solicit fees for ministry other than as provided by law.

5. Clergy may have control of a discretionary fund, not otherwise specifically designated or under the control of an assembly, which they may apply as they see fit to lawful and pious causes.

Principle 86: Financial regulation

1. Regulation of finance in a church is set out in its general law.

2. Oversight of finance in an ecclesiastical unit in a church resides in its assembly or other designated authority.

3. Day-to-day administration of funds by a lawfully constituted financial executive is subject to the general direction and control of the relevant assembly to the extent provided by law.

4. The bishop has no unilateral general control over finance within the diocese.

5. Funds must be used according to the terms of any gift by which they are acquired.

6. A church may make provision for the investigation of complaints of financial mismanagement to be carried out by an independent body with an appeal lying to an appropriate ecclesiastical authority.

Principle 87: Church offerings

1. Ministers must instruct the faithful in their responsibilities towards the missionary work of the church, and give suitable opportunity for offerings to maintain that work.

2. The faithful should make financial offerings according to their means.

3. The duty to collect offerings at the time of public worship vests in wardens.

4. The disbursement of income from offerings is to be determined by a church assembly or other lawful authority.

5. Fees payable on the performance of such ecclesiastical ministrations as marriage and burials may be levied to the extent and in the manner prescribed by church law.

Principle 88: Diocesan and parish shares

1. A diocese should make a financial contribution to the national, regional or provincial church to fund activities undertaken at these levels.

2. A parish should contribute, through its assembly, a parish share or other such payment towards the finances of the diocese.

3. A church may make legal provision as to the diocesan and parish share for: the duty to pay; the assessment of the sum due, which should be fair and equitable; the timing of payment; appeals against the assessment; and sanctions for non-payment.

Principle 89: Responsible investment

1. Church trustees may make such financial investments as are authorised by law.

2. Investments should be not only financially prudent but morally sound.

3. Powers of investment enjoyed by trustees at all levels of a church are to be exercised subject to the lawful direction and control of an ecclesiastical assembly.

4. Trustees are not liable personally for any financial loss resulting from an investment unless such loss is due to their own default or negligence as established by civil law.

Principle 90: Insurance and risk

1. Church assemblies, officers and other church bodies should be aware of the risks associated with their activities.

2. Church property, real and personal, and its occupation and usage, and individual church officers and activities should be insured as appropriate against loss, damage and injury.

3. A church should identify the ecclesiastical bodies or persons with a duty to insure, use insurers of proven competence and specify the extent of the insurance required.

4. Insurance policies should be regularly reviewed.

Principle 91: Maintenance of ministry: stipends

1. When ministry, ordained or lay, is full-time, it should be maintained financially by means of a stipend or other form of remuneration.

2. Stipend funds may be held and administered at a national, regional, provincial, diocesan or other level provided by law.

3. Stipend rates may be determined by a national, regional, provincial, diocesan or parish assembly as provided by law.

4. Provision for non-stipendiary ordained ministry may be made within a church.

5. A church should make provision for the recurrent expenses of ministers.

Principle 92: Care in retirement: pensions and retirement benefits

1. A church should provide financial support for clergy during their retirement.

2. Ministers in receipt of a stipend are entitled to a pension upon their retirement on the basis of contributions made to or membership of a clergy pension fund.

3. A clergy pension fund should be set up at national, regional or provincial level.

4. A clergy pension fund should provide for pensions on retirement, maintenance for spouses and dependants, and awards during periods of disability or illness.

5. A clergy pension fund is administered by trustees accountable to a church.

6. Trustees of a clergy pension fund must keep audited accounts and make an annual report on the administration of the fund to the appropriate ecclesiastical authority.

7. Trustees are not personally liable for losses to a clergy pension fund unless such losses are the result of their own wilful default or culpable negligence.

8. A proper actuarial relationship should be maintained between contributions made to, levied and collected for, and the several benefits paid from, a clergy pension fund or plan.

9. A church may provide pension arrangements for lay employees of ecclesiastical entities.

10. Retirement benefits, retirement funds and retirement payments may be provided in place of pension provision as appropriate.

Part VIII: Ecumenical Relations

The modern ecumenical movement—oriented towards the re-establishment of the visible unity of all Christian people in the one church—developed in the course of the late nineteenth and twentieth centuries. Early on, the Anglican commitment to ecumenism was articulated by the 1888 Lambeth Conference (Resolution 11):

> *That, in the opinion of this Conference, the following articles supply a basis on which approach may be by God's blessing made towards Home Reunion:*
>
> *a. The Holy Scriptures of the Old and New Testaments, as 'containing all things necessary to salvation,' and as being the rule and ultimate standard of faith.*
>
> *b. The Apostles' Creed, as the baptismal symbol; and the Nicene Creed, as the sufficient statement of the Christian faith.*
>
> *c. The two sacraments ordained by Christ himself—Baptism and the Supper of the Lord—ministered with unfailing use of Christ's words of institution, and of the elements ordained by him.*
>
> *d. The historic episcopate, locally adapted in the methods of its administration to the varying needs of the nations and peoples called of God into the unity of his Church.*

The Anglican Communion has never seen itself as a complete and self-sufficient entity, but as an expression of Communion within the One, Holy, Catholic and Apostolic Church, which takes seriously its vocation to reach out beyond its own life to the greater unity of the church. The course of the twentieth century saw this vision applied in real initiatives for ecumenical cooperation, including schemes of shared mission and unity. This in turn stimulated the growth of a body of legal instruments in the churches which sought to facilitate and order ecumenical engagement and commitment. In part giving expression to the various ecumenical agreements and covenants, and in part seeking to enable and equip Anglicans for ecumenical endeavour, canon law concentrates on the application of the theology of κοινωνια *(communion), which undergirds much of the ecumenical movement, and addresses in the main issues of ecclesial communion and reciprocal membership and participation.*

Principle 93: Ecumenical responsibility

1. The church universal is indivisible, and it is the will of God that separated churches should share a more visible communion than exists one with another.

2. The mission of a church is part of the wider mission of all Christians.

3. A church should promote mutual understanding, foster reciprocal fellowship, seek ecumenical cooperation and strive for visible unity among the separated churches.

Principle 94: Ecclesial communion

1. Ecclesial communion between two or more churches exists when a relationship is established in which each church believes the other to hold the essentials of the Christian faith and recognises the apostolicity of the other.

2. Full communion involves the recognition of unity in faith, sacramental sharing, the mutual recognition and interchangeability of ministries, and the reciprocal enjoyment of shared spiritual, pastoral, liturgical and collegial resources.

3. Inter-communion is an ecclesial relationship in which at least one but not all of the elements of full communion are present.

4. Churches in communion with each other remain autonomous but share interdependence with regard to those matters and as defined in the instrument governing their relationship of communion.

5. The relationship of communion does not require the acceptance of all theological opinion, sacramental devotion or liturgical practice characteristic of another church.

Principle 95: Ecumenical freedom

1. A church is free to establish relations of ecclesial communion with churches not in the Anglican Communion as permitted by the discipline of each ecumenical partner.

2. It is for a church in agreement with its ecumenical partner to determine when dialogue reaches a stage which allows establishment of ecclesial communion.

3. If a member church of the Anglican Communion enters a relation of ecclesial communion with a non-member church, this effects a relationship between such non-member church and other member churches of the Anglican Communion only to the extent provided in their own laws and the regulatory instruments of the non-member church.

Principle 96: Ecclesial recognition

1. Ecumenical relations may be authorised centrally and administered locally.

2. The authority in a member church of the Anglican Communion to recognise a non-member church, in order to establish ecumenical relations, vests in its central assembly or other lawfully designated body, and such authority shall be exercised in such manner as may be prescribed by the law of that church.

3. A church may establish commissions with such membership and functions as may be prescribed under its law to enable ecumenism by stages or other process.

Principle 97: Ecumenical agreements

1. The extent and terms of ecclesial communion or other relationship between a church and a church not in the Anglican Communion may be set out in a constitutional union, concordat, covenant or other instrument agreed between the participant churches.

2. A church may incorporate in its own law an ecumenical instrument to which it is party in order to implement the terms of ministerial, liturgical or sacramental communion or other form of reciprocity as agreed by the participant churches.

3. A parish may enter a local ecumenical project to provide for shared ministerial, liturgical or sacramental communion or other form of reciprocity agreed by the participant churches, in the manner and to the extent authorised by law.

Principle 98: Ecumenical collaboration

1. For the visible unity to which Christ calls all the faithful, ministers should seek to foster and participate in ecumenical partnership with faith communities of other Christian traditions, especially those with which their church already has formal relations, to the extent permitted by the discipline of each church involved.

2. Ministers should in ecumenical affairs collaborate, cooperate and where appropriate consult with ministers of other faith communities and in all

dealings with them act courteously and with respect for their corporate traditions.

3. Ministers (a) should minister to members of other faith communities if authorised by the discipline of their own church and of the other community; and (b) should not solicit membership of their own church from a member of another faith community.

4. If called upon to provide ministry, such as pastoral care or at a baptism, wedding or funeral, for persons belonging to another faith community, ministers should as appropriate (a) suggest they approach a minister of that other community; (b) consult with a minister of that community for advice; and (c) consult within their own church.

5. Ministers may approach colleagues in another faith community to minister to a member of their own church only in exceptional cases at the request of that member.

Principle 99: Reception

1. Baptism is a basic requirement for reception into a church.

2. When a baptised person from another church not in the Anglican Communion, but holding the apostolic faith, desires communicant membership, a priest, if assured of such desire, should after due preparation present that person to the bishop for reception at the time of confirmation or some other convenient time.

3. A person may be received into membership of a church by the rite of confirmation or by such other means as may be authorised for this purpose according to the law of that church.

4. The reception of a person should be recorded in the registers of a church.

Principle 100: Eucharistic hospitality

1. Communicant members of a church may receive Holy Communion in a church not in the Anglican Communion which subscribes to the doctrine of the Holy Trinity and upholds the apostolic faith, in such circumstances as are permitted by the discipline both of their own church and of the host church.

2. There may be admitted to the Holy Communion in a church, to the extent permitted by its discipline, baptised persons who are communicant members of good standing in a church not in the Anglican Communion which upholds the apostolic faith subscribing to the doctrine of the Holy Trinity.

3. The competent authority within a church should present the normal requirements for membership of that church to any person who regularly receives Holy Communion over a long period likely to continue indefinitely when such person is from a church not in the Anglican Communion but which upholds the apostolic faith and subscribes to the doctrine of the Holy Trinity.

A Reflection on the Common Principles of Canon Law

By the Rt Revd Dr Vicentia Kgabe, Bishop of Lesotho, Anglican Church of Southern Africa

A great deal of work has been carried out by so many people since 2001 when the Primates of the Anglican Communion first welcomed the idea of articulating common principles of canon law derived from what the churches of the worldwide Anglican Communion share in their laws. The Anglican Communion's Network of Legal Advisers, established under the auspices of the Anglican Consultative Council, took up the challenge and from 2002 to 2008 worked hard on the project resulting in the launch of *The Principles of Canon Law Common to the Churches of the Anglican Communion* at the Lambeth Conference 2008. In what follows I reflect on canon law and on the second iteration of the document, which is to be unveiled at the Lambeth Conference in 2022.

Like its predecessor, the 2022 document sets out to describe general patterns of church life to be found in the many regulatory instruments, from constitutions through canons to liturgical and other norms, of churches across the Communion. The aim of the document is to inform Anglicans and the wider world of what they share legally—and of course the laws from which these principles are derived themselves express shared Anglican theological understandings. Its aim is not to oblige. It is a statement of principles of law, not of laws, on the basis that only each church has capacity to make laws, and then for itself only. As Anglicans, we have found commonality in the shared fundamentals of our laws and so can point to another 'instrument', alongside our cherished and well-established 'bonds of affection', that binds us together by revealing our shared identity and polity. It was because the 2008 document was so highly valued, in being used, reflected upon and applied in contexts where the laws of churches may have been silent, as well as because of the changes that have been made to church laws since 2008, that the revision was embarked upon. For me personally, it has been an invaluable learning opportunity and an honour to serve the Communion in being part of the revision of the document over this past year.

In March 2022 I attended a seminar on church governance. A presenter made a statement that has stayed with me and is now something of a mantra for me. He said: 'The church is governed by law and not by whimsy.' This expresses in a nutshell the fundamental idea that law is central to and a necessary element in the life of the church. The law of each church in our Communion is itself the by-product, the servant, of so much that is key to the life, mission and witness of the church. Christian belief is the primary source of law; action is the primary focus of law; and serving God and the world is the primary end of law. In these senses, the law of each church is a place of real theological reflection translated into ecclesial practice.

Seeing the law in these ways, I have come to know and love the Anglican Communion with its imperfections. Law does not displace theology and the fundamental spiritual character of the churches and their work. Law does not negate our ability to worship, or frustrate our spirituality, or hinder us in living out our faith in the various contexts in which we are located. Nor does church law take away our commissioning to be alive to God's presence wherever we are. The law simply acts as a guide in the ministries to which both lay and ordained people are all called.

It has taken me a long time to embrace this understanding and appreciation of church law. When I was a teenager, many a time when I heard the 'canons' mentioned I thought something was wrong or someone was in trouble, and in most cases that someone was the priest. However, this was an incomplete perception on my part. Yes, many laws are made to maintain order, to prevent wrongdoing and to remedy it. But they do so to facilitate integrity in the public life of the church as it regulates itself for the common good of its members and wider world. Archbishop Rowan Williams put it well in the foreword to the 2008 document: 'law, properly understood, is not an alien imposition on a grumbling public but a way of securing two things for the common good … the first is consistency … the second is clarity about responsibility'.

My next encounter with church law was at a diocesan clergy meeting. I was attending as an ordinand. A diocesan official addressed the clergy on the constitution and canons. What I remember is feeling fearful of getting into any kind of trouble or making a mistake because 'the canons' would be applied, and that would be the end of any ministry I exercised. I did not see or sense grace as being relevant to church law. All I saw was the law coming down hard on anyone who fails to uphold it. There was also an exclusiveness about the constitution and canons. They were meant only for the ordained; only the clergy had copies of them, and only the clergy could 'decode' them. They were not for the whole church and all its people. Indeed, the popular practices and customs, handed down orally from one church generation to the next, are not found in the constitution and canons. And so, when a direction was needed from the canons, or disciplinary processes were carried out, only then would people realise that there are canons and that they supersede whatever local rules formal or informal have been used in practice.

As a result of all of these perceptions and experiences, whether they were correct or not, as a layperson discerning a calling to holy orders and later serving the church as an ordained person, I resolved to learn more about the constitution and canons. After ordination the need to learn became more pressing: it would be essential to know the rules of ministry once I was entrusted by the church to lead and care for the faithful. It was not enough simply to own a copy of the constitution and canons of the Anglican Church of Southern Africa, and my vow of canonical obedience required more learning. This learning process would include thinking about them theologically, embodying them in the practice of ministry, recognising how pervasive they are across the whole of my ministry and developing a critical and reflective attitude towards them.

In turn, I enrolled on the part-time postgraduate Master of Laws (LLM) course in Canon Law at the Cardiff Law School in Wales. This has allowed me to learn what law is, who makes it and how, and with what purpose and effects. Above all, students are encouraged to be able competently to describe, explain and evaluate Anglican law in its wider theological, historical, civil and ecumenical contexts. This is where I was introduced to *The Principles of Canon Law Common to the Churches of the Anglican Communion*, a project which itself began as a Cardiff initiative. It has taught me, not least, to make sense of and flesh out Canon 50 of the Anglican Church of Southern Africa, which, on 'the interpretation of the laws and canons of this Church', provides:

> It is hereby declared that if any question should arise as to the interpretation of the canons or laws of this Church, or of any part thereof, the interpretation shall be governed by *the general principles of Canon Law* thereto applicable. [Emphasis added]

The project is not rocket science. The church has used juristic axioms, maxims or principles for over a thousand years. They were descriptive and prescriptive in form, used in teaching to sum up the details of clusters of particular rules of church law, and they often sought to mirror the fundamentals of the Christian faith and life. Their modern value continues. The Anglican project itself has been used in Anglican–Roman Catholic dialogue and as a model for the wider ecumenical movement in global Christianity with the *Statement of Principles of Christian Law* (Rome, 2016), today being fed into the faith and order work of the World Council of Churches.

This is the principal value of the second iteration of the principles document—to function as a unifying force for global Anglicanism through the experience of common enquiry, study and expression. The principles of Anglican canon law are at the centre of a table at which I have been given a once-in-a-lifetime opportunity to sit: a table at which I witnessed the best of the Anglican Communion displayed—with lawyers and theologians, clergy and laypersons, practitioners and scholars working together for the common good of the Anglican Communion. First, there were the meetings within the Anglican Church of Southern Africa. We met virtually, we unpacked the principles, and we consulted our own regulatory instruments for consistency. Second, in the revision committee, the submissions of each church were treated with care and respect, differences were aired, a new understanding was gained. The revision process was not rushed, because we knew that all the churches across the Communion spent weeks and months looking at their own laws and seeking to see whether these were consistent with the principles on offer.

I believe that the value of the document *The Principles of Canon Law Common to the Churches of the Anglican Communion* is undeniable. The potentialities of this whole project are summed up in the idea of 'maximising' church laws for Anglican unity. Not only does the 2022 second edition 'maximise' the laws themselves, in the sense of presenting laws and the changes in them since 2008 in the form of principles or maxims. It also seeks to maximise or increase the potential of each church through its own lawmaking and its own legal instruments as forms of applied theology, in order to contribute to the fruits of global Anglican unity.

I hope my journey with learning about canon law, and especially the principles of canon law common to the churches of the Anglican Communion, will inspire many across our churches.

Appendix:
Revisions between 2008 and 2022

Listed below are the principles which have been revised between 2008 and 2022.

There have been four kinds of revision: additions, deletions, amendments and relocations. Where the number of a principle alone is given, this indicates that the 2008 principle has been amended without any change in numbering. Where a principle from 2008 has been deleted or relocated this is indicated using the prefix 2008/ before the number of the principle. Where a principle new to the 2022 revision has been added this is indicated by the prefix 2022/. The details of each revision can be studied by comparing the 2008 and 2022 publications.

Added to the Definitions section in 2022: 'Anglican Communion', 'Civil law', 'may', 'to the extent provided by law'.

Part I
2.2, 3.2.

Part II
Preamble, 11.4, 12.7, 13.5.

Part III
15.10, 15.11, 17.1, 18.2, 24.9.

Part IV
Preamble, 30.12, 32.7, 32.8, 35.2, 36.1, 37.7, 2008/38.5 relocated to preamble, 39.2, 39.7, 40.2, 41.4, 41.5, 42.4, 43.6, 47.2.

Part V

48.7, 49.5, 2008/50.5 deleted, 53.5, 54.2, 54.6, 55.1, 55.4, 55.6, 58.2, 58.3, 60.1.

Part VI

Preamble, 61.5, 65.5, 66.2, 66.3, 69.2, 69.3, 69.5, 69.9, 70, 72.4, 72.5, 73.1, 73.2, 73.5, 73.6, 74.2, 74.3, 75.1, 75.3, 75.5, 2008/75.10 deleted, 76.6, 77, 78.1, 79.2, 79.4, 79.5, 79.6.

Part VII

80.2, 82.1, 83.1, 83.5, 84.1, 86.2, 86.3, 86.6, 87.4, 89.3, 89.4, 91.1, 2008/91.2 deleted, 92.2, 92.6, 92.8, 2022/92.9 added, 2022/92.10 added.

Part VIII

94.4, 96.3, 100.2, 100.3

Index

Made in United States
Troutdale, OR
08/06/2026

52510928R00096